Planet Earth

TIME-LIFE
ALEXANDRIA, VIRGINIA

CONTENTS

5 Rock of Ages   84

6 Harvesting Earth's Mineral Bounty   96

7 The Oceans: Sculptors of the Planet   108

1

This Majestic Planet

Of all the planets in the Solar System, Earth alone had the good fortune to form neither too close to the Sun nor too far away from it. As a result, Earth became the only planet with temperatures that permit the existence of abundant liquid water.

These wet, moderate conditions were ideal for the development of various life forms, the first of which appeared just 1.5 billion years or so after the planet's creation. Eons and eons of evolution eventually produced intelligent beings who began to wonder about the place they called home. More than 2,000 years ago, for example, Greek philosophers deduced that the Earth was a sphere; final proof of this came when Magellan's ships circumnavigated the globe in the 16th century. And in the 20th century, satellite views like the one at right revealed the planet as a beautiful blue orb floating in space.

The inside of the Earth, however, remains an unseen mystery. Unseen, but not unknowable: Using seismic waves and magnetic fields as indirect probes of the planet's interior, scientists have discovered that the planet consists of three main layers: the crust, the mantle, and the core. These layers harbor great energy, which can surface violently as earthquakes and volcanoes but is also responsible for the formation of mountain ranges and valuable mineral deposits. In short, the seemingly solid surface of Earth is merely the covering of a seething, dynamic cauldron of energy and matter.

A composite image from a weather satellite reveals the grandeur and beauty of planet Earth. Though often called a sphere, Earth is technically an oblate spheroid. The centrifugal force of its rotation has slightly flattened the planet at its poles.

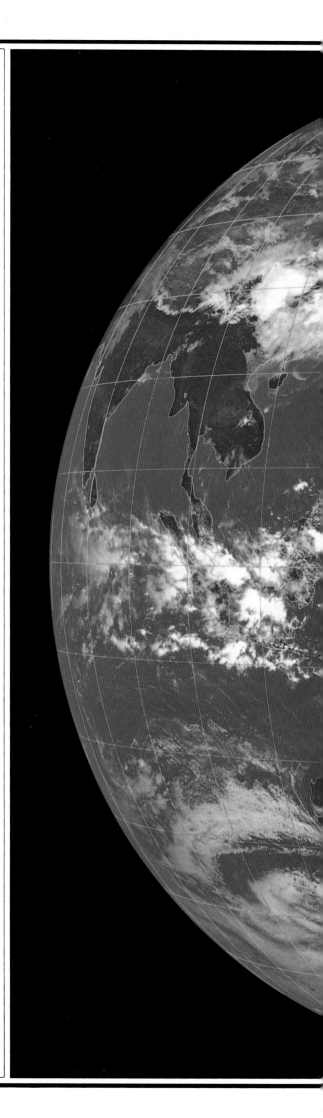

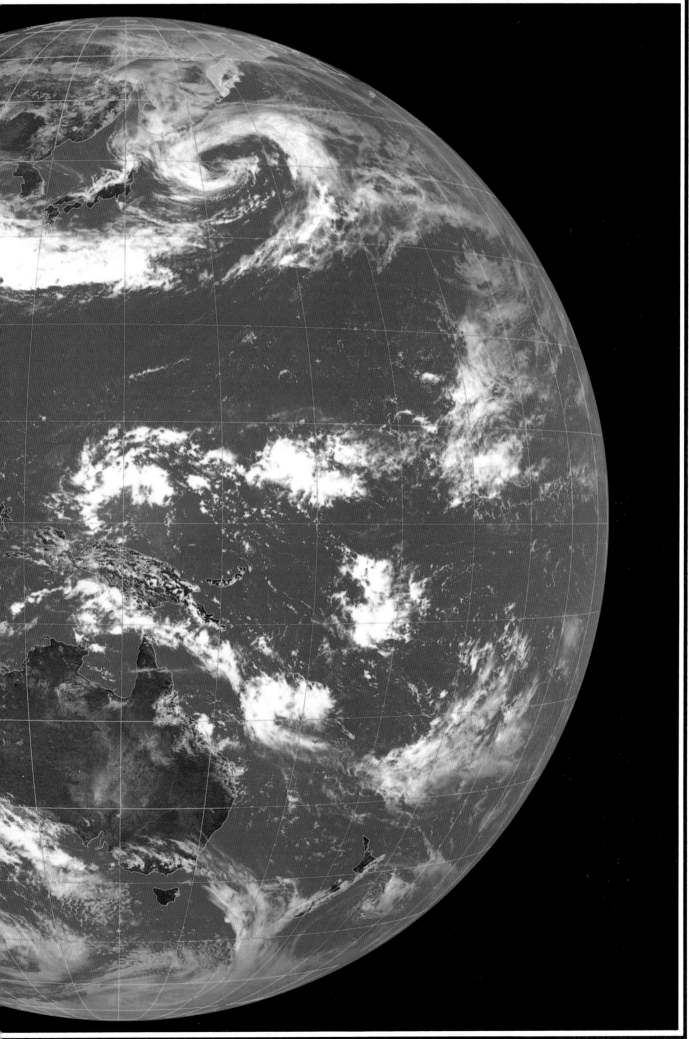

How Did the Earth Form?

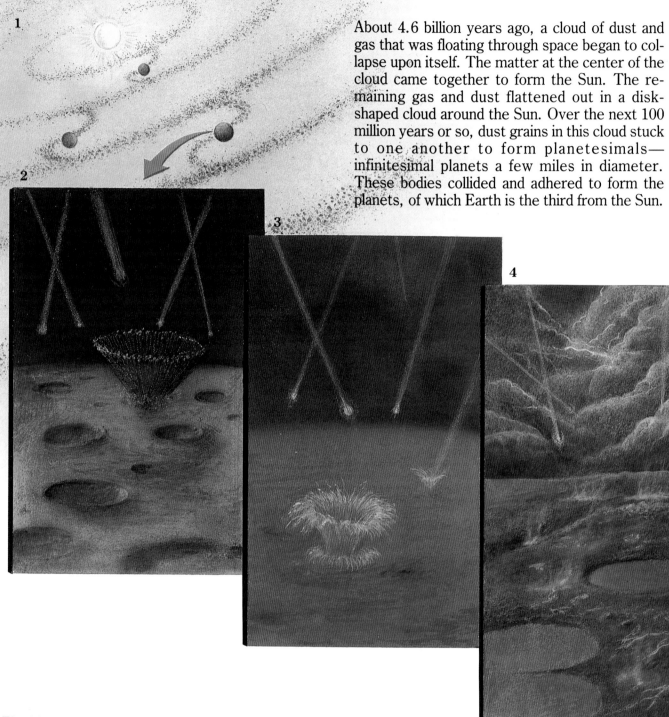

About 4.6 billion years ago, a cloud of dust and gas that was floating through space began to collapse upon itself. The matter at the center of the cloud came together to form the Sun. The remaining gas and dust flattened out in a disk-shaped cloud around the Sun. Over the next 100 million years or so, dust grains in this cloud stuck to one another to form planetesimals—infinitesimal planets a few miles in diameter. These bodies collided and adhered to form the planets, of which Earth is the third from the Sun.

The birth of Earth

1. Earth began to take shape when grains of dust in the flat cloud around the Sun started to stick together. Clumps of these particles built up into larger bodies; these in turn collided to create planet-size objects.
2. Debris from the original cloud rained down on the young world. The energy from this infalling material, along with heating from radioactive decay, caused the Earth to melt.
3. As a result of this melting, dense materials—chiefly iron—sank to the center of the planet to form the core. Earth's surface was covered by a sea of molten rock. Lighter materials such as water vapor and carbon dioxide migrated outward to form a primitive atmosphere.
4. The solar wind—a high-speed stream of charged parti-

cles from the Sun—swept the Solar System clean of debris, so impacts on Earth decreased. The planet cooled, and water vapor formed dense clouds in the atmosphere.
5. The clouds cooled, their water vapor condensed, and torrential rains inundated Earth. Gradually the downpour cooled the rocks on the surface.
6. Runoff from the storms collected in low-lying places, creating the beginnings of the world's oceans. Carbon dioxide from the air began to dissolve in these immense pools, further cooling the planet.
7. By about 2.5 billion years ago, the blue Earth had emerged from the chaos of creation. The clouds dissipated and the Sun shone on a world much like the one of today.

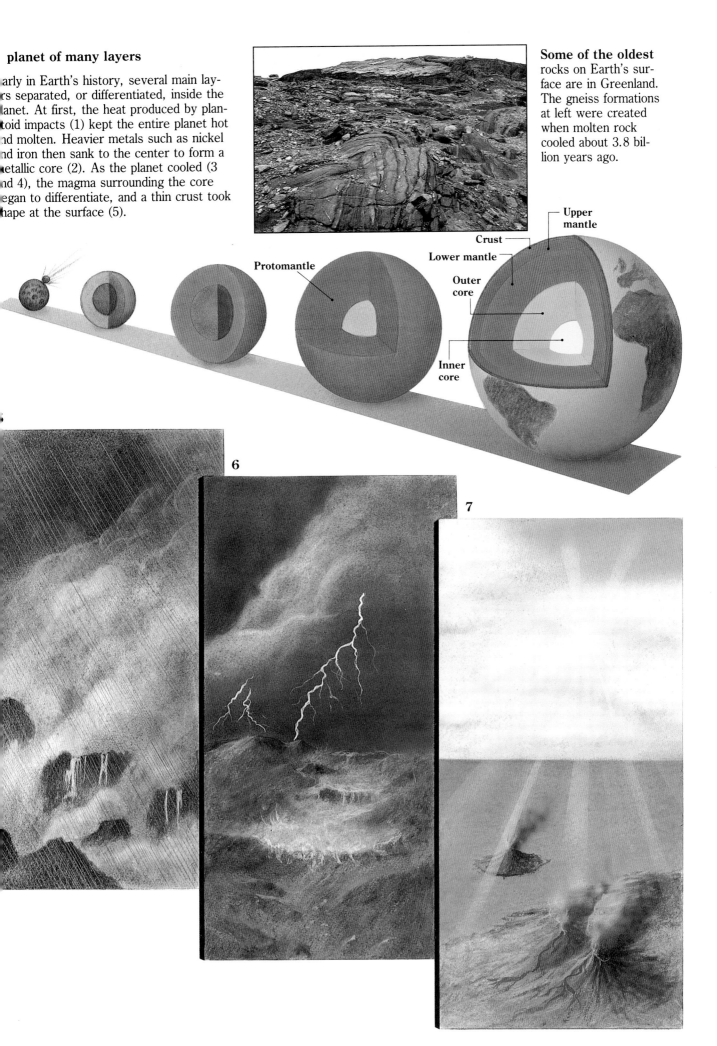

planet of many layers

Early in Earth's history, several main layers separated, or differentiated, inside the planet. At first, the heat produced by plantoid impacts (1) kept the entire planet hot and molten. Heavier metals such as nickel and iron then sank to the center to form a metallic core (2). As the planet cooled (3 and 4), the magma surrounding the core began to differentiate, and a thin crust took shape at the surface (5).

Some of the oldest rocks on Earth's surface are in Greenland. The gneiss formations at left were created when molten rock cooled about 3.8 billion years ago.

Protomantle

Crust

Upper mantle

Lower mantle

Outer core

Inner core

6

7

What's inside the Earth?

The structure of the Earth resembles that of an egg: The core is the yolk, the mantle is the white, and the crust is the shell. Compared with the size of the planet, the crust is extremely thin; it ranges from just 5 miles thick on the ocean floor to about 40 miles thick beneath mountain ranges. Below the crust is the mantle, which extends to a depth of some 1,800 miles. The mantle is divided into two layers. Rock in the upper mantle, though largely solid, is very hot and capable of viscous flow—somewhat like hot tar on a summer street. Rock in the lower mantle is more rigid and dense because of the greater pressure at that depth. The nickel-iron core consists of a fluid outer layer and a solid inner core.

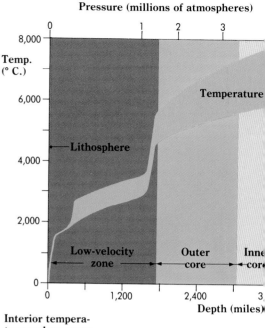

Interior temperature and pressure

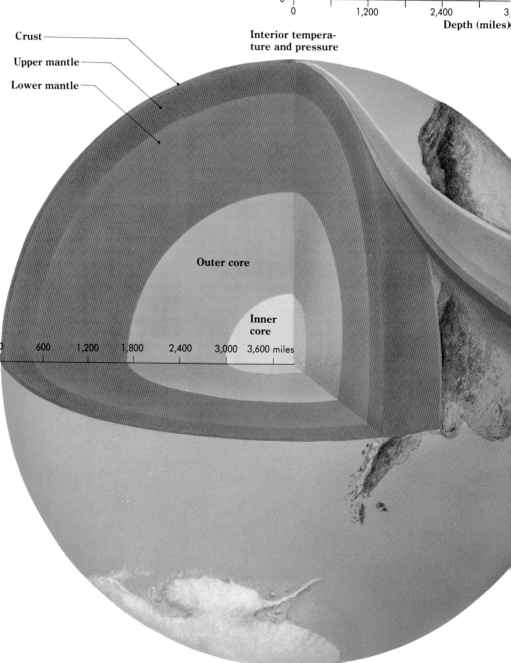

Crust
Upper mantle
Lower mantle

Outer core

Inner core

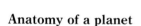
0   600   1,200   1,800   2,400   3,000   3,600 miles

Anatomy of a planet

The crust is thick beneath continents but thin beneath oceans. Near the surface, the continental crust is made up mostly of granite; lower down, it contains mainly basalt. The oceanic crust is primarily basalt.

The mantle envelops the core and constitutes 85 percent of Earth's volume. The low-velocity zone—so named because it slows down seismic waves—is 45 to 125 miles deep. Though solid, the mantle behaves like a slow-moving fluid over long periods of time.

The core, which produces Earth's magnetic field, may reach 12,000° F., with pressures two million times that of Earth's surface.

Layers of the mantle

The rocky upper layer of the mantle and the crust are together called the lithosphere, or "sphere of stone." It is made up of plates that move, creating continental drift. Under the lithosphere is a layer of less rigid rock known as the asthenosphere, or "sphere of weakness." The asthenosphere holds pockets of molten mantle, which has high temperatures and a viscous condition that tend to slow down seismic waves. For this reason, the asthenosphere is often called the low-velocity zone.

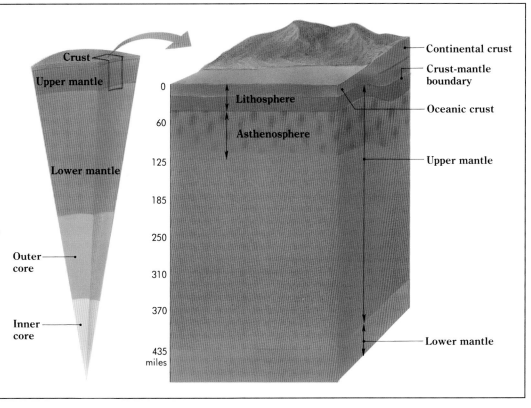

Crust
Upper mantle
Lower mantle
Outer core
Inner core

Lithosphere
Asthenosphere

0
60
125
185
250
310
370
435 miles

Continental crust
Crust-mantle boundary
Oceanic crust
Upper mantle
Lower mantle

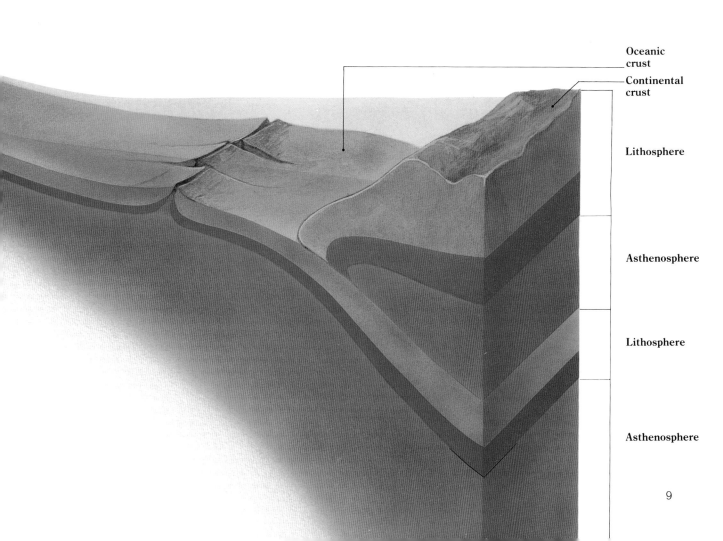

Oceanic crust
Continental crust
Lithosphere
Asthenosphere
Lithosphere
Asthenosphere

9

What Is the Crust Made Of?

The Earth's crust is not the same thickness everywhere. Over the continents, the crust is an average of 20 miles thick; over the oceans, by contrast, it is just 3 to 5 miles thick.

In addition to being thicker than the oceanic crust, the continental crust is more varied. Its upper layers consist of light, granitic rocks, while its lower layers are made of denser basaltic rocks. These layers—or strata, as geologists call them—were formed at different times by a range

of processes. The oldest rocks are found in the Precambrian shields. Younger rocks formed during eras of mountain building.

The oceanic crust is hidden by the seas, but geologists have determined that its top stratum is sediment up to half a mile thick. Constantly being reformed by volcanic eruptions along undersea vents known as mid-ocean ridges, the oceanic crust is a geologic youngster: It is less than 200 million years old.

Two types of crust

The continental crust, composed of light granitic rocks, rises to higher elevations than the heavier basalt of the oceanic crust. The average elevation of the continental crust is 2,800 feet above sea level, whereas the oceanic crust averages 12,500 feet below sea level. Wind and rain continually erode the continental crust, creating

sand, silt, and clay that eventually wash into the ocean to form a thick layer of sediment on the seafloor. Eruptions along the volcanically active mid-ocean ridges constantly create new oceanic crust; as a result, the oceanic crust is much younger than the continental crust, which is more than 3.8 billion years old in some places.

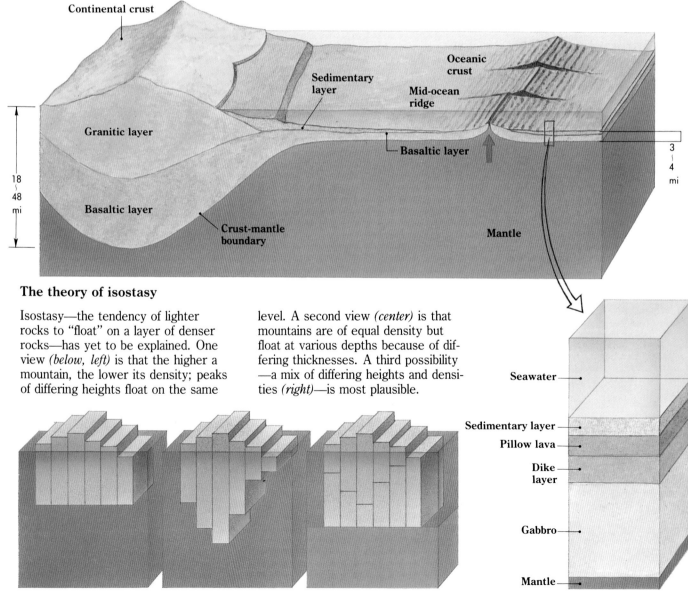

The theory of isostasy

Isostasy—the tendency of lighter rocks to "float" on a layer of denser rocks—has yet to be explained. One view *(below, left)* is that the higher a mountain, the lower its density; peaks of differing heights float on the same

level. A second view *(center)* is that mountains are of equal density but float at various depths because of differing thicknesses. A third possibility —a mix of differing heights and densities *(right)*—is most plausible.

ow continents are made—and moved

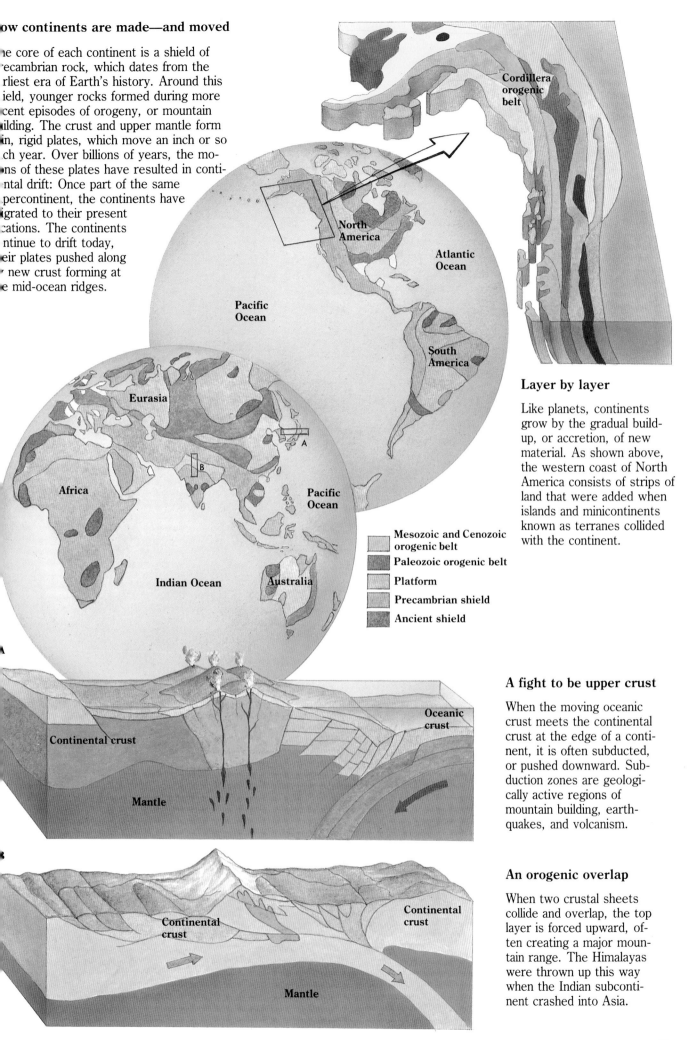

he core of each continent is a shield of
recambrian rock, which dates from the
rliest era of Earth's history. Around this
ield, younger rocks formed during more
cent episodes of orogeny, or mountain
ilding. The crust and upper mantle form
in, rigid plates, which move an inch or so
ch year. Over billions of years, the mo-
ns of these plates have resulted in conti-
ntal drift: Once part of the same
percontinent, the continents have
igrated to their present
cations. The continents
ntinue to drift today,
eir plates pushed along
 new crust forming at
e mid-ocean ridges.

Cordillera
orogenic
belt

North
America

Atlantic
Ocean

Pacific
Ocean

South
America

Eurasia

A

B

Africa

Pacific
Ocean

Indian Ocean

Australia

☐ Mesozoic and Cenozoic
orogenic belt

☐ Paleozoic orogenic belt

☐ Platform

☐ Precambrian shield

☐ Ancient shield

Oceanic
crust

Continental crust

Mantle

Continental
crust

Continental
crust

Mantle

Layer by layer

Like planets, continents
grow by the gradual buildup, or accretion, of new
material. As shown above,
the western coast of North
America consists of strips of
land that were added when
islands and minicontinents
known as terranes collided
with the continent.

A fight to be upper crust

When the moving oceanic
crust meets the continental
crust at the edge of a continent, it is often subducted,
or pushed downward. Sub-
duction zones are geologically active regions of
mountain building, earth-
quakes, and volcanism.

An orogenic overlap

When two crustal sheets
collide and overlap, the top
layer is forced upward, often creating a major mountain range. The Himalayas
were thrown up this way
when the Indian subconti-
nent crashed into Asia.

11

Is Earth Heated from Within?

The sun is not the only source of Earth's warmth. Heat also reaches the surface from deep inside the planet. This heat is produced by the breakdown of the radioactive elements uranium, thorium, and potassium, and by energy that was generated—and then trapped far below the crust—during the planet's formation. The amount of heat (measured in calories) that seeps from the interior each year is 1,000 times greater than the energy produced annually by earthquakes around the world. Averaged over the Earth's surface, however, this heat flow is just .015 calorie per square meter per second. The release of internal heat is most apparent where the crust is thinnest, such as in Iceland, New Zealand, and Wyoming.

Where the crust is thin, the mantle heats surface water, forming hot springs.

Earth's central-heating system

Earth's immense reservoir of internal heat built up early in the planet's formation. Collisions between planetesimals released intense heat; so too did the separation of the metal core from the stony mantle, when temperatures on the planet reached the melting point of iron. Heat was also generated by the pressure of the planet's outer layers and by the disintegration of radioactive elements. Earth's surface then cooled, trapping this primordial heat inside. Today, the heat continues to work its way to the surface, where it causes volcanic eruptions, geysers, earthquakes, seafloor spreading, continental drift, and the formation of new mountains.

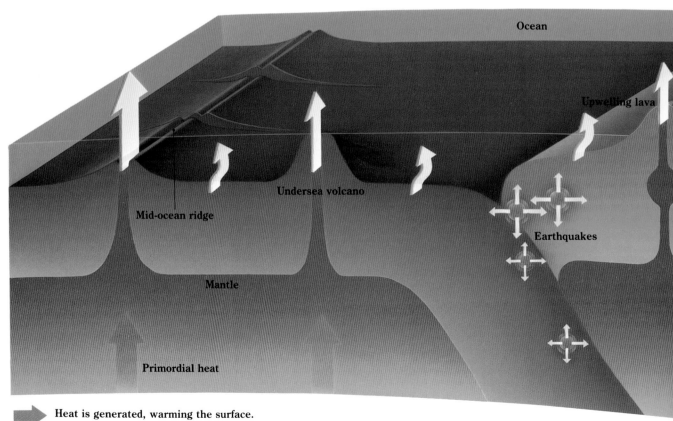

Ocean

Upwelling lava

Undersea volcano

Mid-ocean ridge

Earthquakes

Mantle

Primordial heat

➡ Heat is generated, warming the surface.

➡ Heat dissipates, cooling the interior.

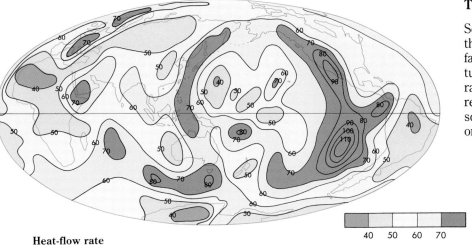

Terrestrial heat flow

Scientists map heat flow from the interior by combining surface and subsurface temperatures with the heat-transfer rates of various rocks. The result is given as calories per square centimeter per second or milliwatts per square meter.

Heat-flow rate

40	50	60	70

As shown on the world map above, heat flow tends to be higher in the oceans than on the continents. The greatest heat flow occurs along the mid-ocean ridges; it lessens as the distance from the ridge increases and is lowest in continental shields. The source of this output differs as well. Continental heat originates from radioactive granite near the surface; heat from the seafloor, which lacks granite, originates deep in the mantle.

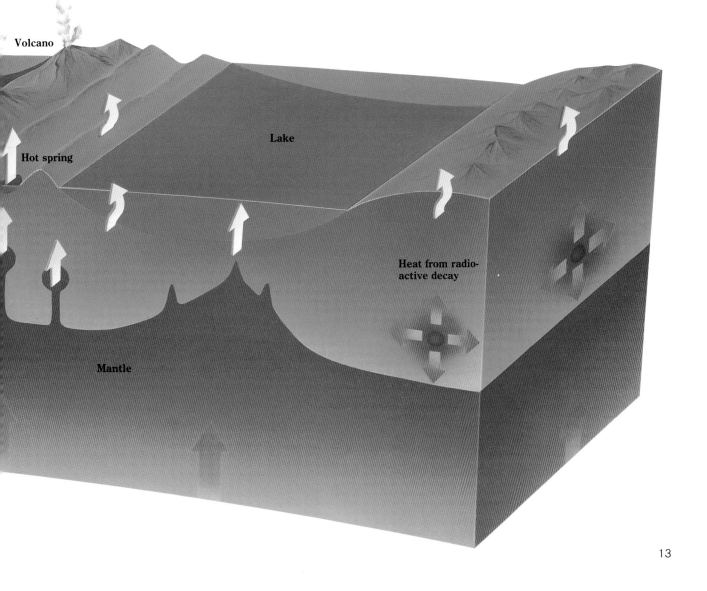

Volcano

Hot spring

Lake

Heat from radioactive decay

Mantle

How Is Earth's Interior Studied?

Although direct observation of Earth's interior is not yet possible—the deepest hole ever drilled extends down only 8 miles—scientists have learned a great deal by studying the vibrations produced by earthquakes. These vibrations, called seismic waves, spread out from a quake's underground focus; upon reaching the surface of the Earth, they are recorded and their intensity is measured.

Studies of the three kinds of seismic waves—surface waves, compressional waves, and shear waves—have revealed a region 9 to 30 miles deep where the waves abruptly slow down. This region is known as the Mohorovičić discontinuity, or Moho, in honor of the Croatian seismologist who discovered it in 1909. The Moho marks a sudden change in the density and other properties of the rocks on either side of it; in fact, it divides the crust from the mantle. Other discontinuities exist at depths of 1,800 and 3,200 miles.

Rather than waiting for earthquakes to occur, scientists often gather data by detonating underground explosives and recording the seismic waves they produce. They also use the technique of seismic tomography to construct three-dimensional models of the Earth's interior.

Seismic waves

When seismic waves hit a discontinuity, or boundary between layers *(right, top),* they pass through it directly or by refraction, or they are reflected from it. The time-distance curves show that direct waves arrive first at stations near the quake because they travel the shortest distance. At stations farther away, the faster-moving refracted waves arrive first. The point at which both waves arrive together indicates the depth of the layer boundary.

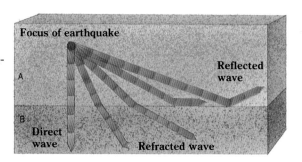

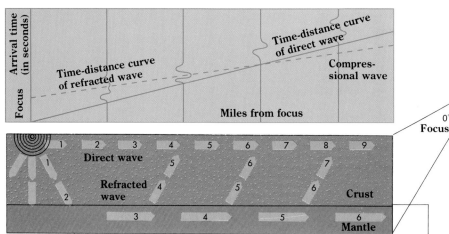

A layered Earth

If Earth's density increased steadily toward the core, seismic waves would travel as shown below at left. But density changes abruptly from one layer to the next, causing seismic waves to be reflected or refracted *(below, right).* This lets geologists gauge each layer's thickness.

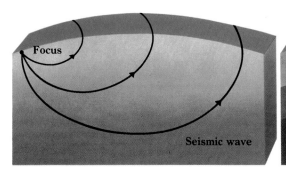

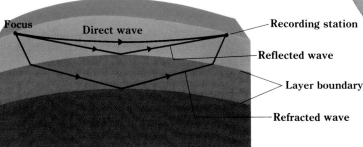

Probing to the core

The technique of seismic tomography records intersecting seismic waves at different locations to create a three-dimensional view of density inside the Earth. In the diagram at far right, the areas in red and yellow are less dense than their surroundings; the areas shown in blue and green are of higher density. The result is a detailed portrait of Earth's inner structure.

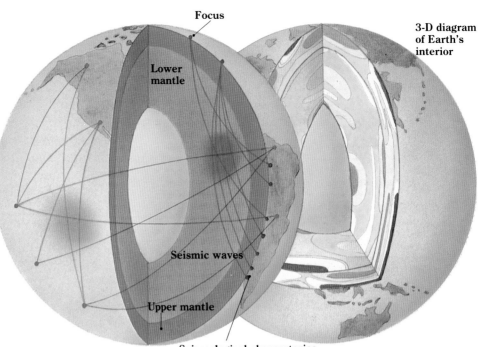

Tremors in the Earth

Earthquakes send shear waves and compressional waves through the globe. When the faster-moving compressional waves reach the inner core, they encounter a sudden increase in density and are refracted, creating a shadow zone unaffected by them. Shear waves never travel through the outer core, nor do they propagate through liquids; scientists have therefore concluded that Earth's outer core consists of material in a liquid state.

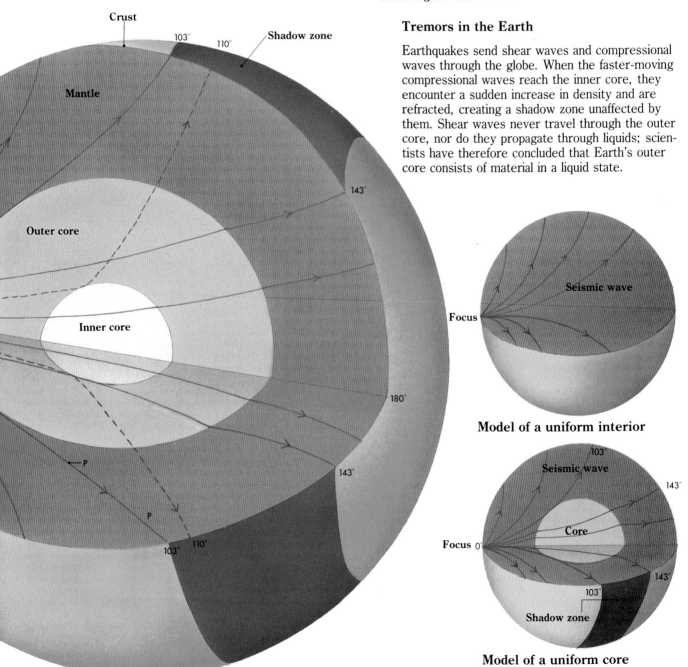

Model of a uniform interior

Model of a uniform core

How Big Is the Earth?

Ever since the fourth century BC, when Greek philosophers determined that the Earth is a sphere, scientists have been trying to measure the planet's size precisely. One famous attempt was made by Eratosthenes, curator of the library in Alexandria, Egypt. In 230 BC, Eratosthenes found that the noontime shadow cast by a vertical rod in his city was longer than the shadow cast at the same moment by an identical rod in the city of Syene, 570 miles to the south. (On a flat Earth, the shadows would be the same length in both cities.) By measuring the difference in the angle between the sun and the two rods, and knowing the distance between the two cities, Eratosthenes was able to calculate the circumference of the Earth at the equator. His result was only 15 percent larger than the true value of 24,900 miles. Measurements taken from space show that the planet is not quite a perfect sphere.

The view from space reveals a spherical Earth. The ancient Greeks used geometry to figure the planet's shape and size.

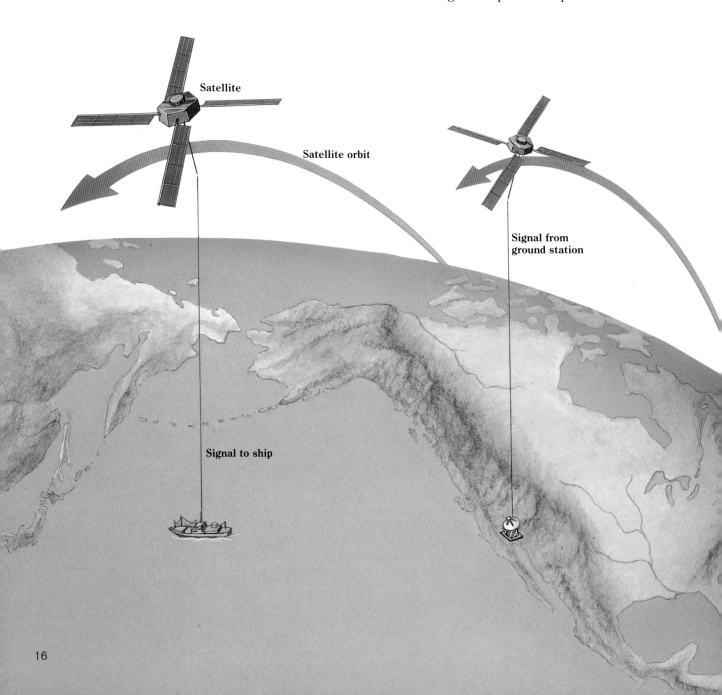

Satellite

Satellite orbit

Signal from ground station

Signal to ship

Calculating the girth of Earth

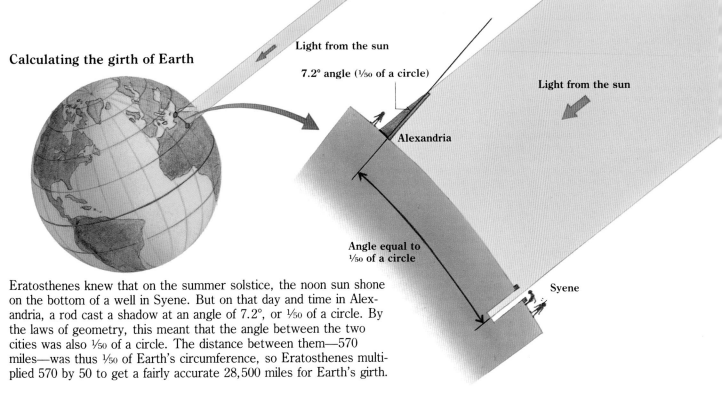

Light from the sun

7.2° angle (¹⁄₅₀ of a circle)

Alexandria

Light from the sun

Angle equal to ¹⁄₅₀ of a circle

Syene

Eratosthenes knew that on the summer solstice, the noon sun shone on the bottom of a well in Syene. But on that day and time in Alexandria, a rod cast a shadow at an angle of 7.2°, or ¹⁄₅₀ of a circle. By the laws of geometry, this meant that the angle between the two cities was also ¹⁄₅₀ of a circle. The distance between them—570 miles—was thus ¹⁄₅₀ of Earth's circumference, so Eratosthenes multiplied 570 by 50 to get a fairly accurate 28,500 miles for Earth's girth.

An imperfect sphere

North Pole

Radius at equator: 3,961 miles

Radius at poles: 3,948 miles

Equator

South Pole

The matter that makes up the Earth is pulled toward the center of the planet by gravity, giving the globe a spherical shape. Centrifugal force created by Earth's rotation, however, causes a slight flattening at the poles. As shown at left, Earth therefore measures 24,901.5 miles around the equator but just 24,859.7 miles around the poles. Ignoring or averaging out such irregularities as mountains and seafloors reveals an Earth-shape, or geoid, that deviates slightly from a perfect ellipsoid.

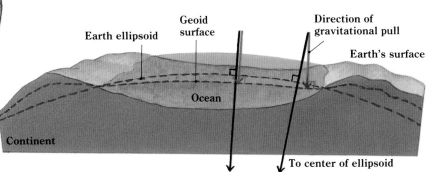

Geoid surface

Direction of gravitational pull

Earth ellipsoid

Earth's surface

Ocean

Continent

To center of ellipsoid

Measurements from space

Measurements from different sites on the ground can pinpoint the location of a satellite orbiting the Earth (left). The satellite's position can then be used to determine the distance between points on Earth, enabling ships at sea to use the satellite as a navigational beacon. No satellite's orbit is entirely symmetrical, however; irregularities in Earth's gravity cause the orbit to vary somewhat. For this reason, satellites can accurately measure Earth's gravitational field. These measurements show the Earth to be slightly pear-shaped (right); the North Pole is 46 feet higher than a perfect ellipsoid, while the South Pole is 79 feet lower.

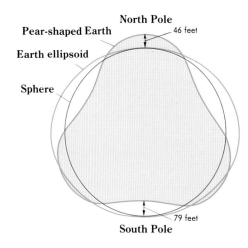

North Pole

Pear-shaped Earth

46 feet

Earth ellipsoid

Sphere

79 feet

South Pole

Does Earth's Gravity Vary?

Gravity is the attractive force between two objects. When someone throws a ball into the air, the planet's superior gravity pulls the ball back to Earth. But objects on Earth are also subject to the centrifugal force created by Earth's rotation on its axis. When a ball tied to a string is swung around, centrifugal force makes the ball fly away from the center of rotation; the longer the string, the stronger the force. On Earth, centrifugal force is greatest at the equator, where the radius of rotation is nearly 4,000 miles, and least at the poles, where the radius of rotation is zero.

The gravitational pull at any spot on Earth is the sum of the attractive force and the centrifugal force exerted on that spot. As a result, the pull of gravity varies slightly with latitude. Altitude and local topography can also cause the Earth's gravity to differ from one place to another nearby.

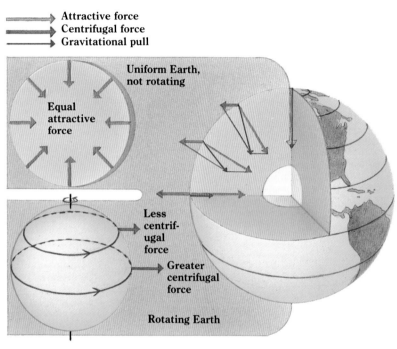

- ⟶ Attractive force
- ⟶ Centrifugal force
- ⟶ Gravitational pull

Uniform Earth, not rotating

Equal attractive force

Less centrifugal force

Greater centrifugal force

Rotating Earth

The effect of latitude on gravity

If the Earth's interior were uniform and the planet did not spin on its axis, the attractive force at the surface would be the same everywhere. On the actual—that is, rotating—Earth, however, centrifugal force declines with increasing latitude, so the apparent pull of gravity is greater at higher latitudes. Measurements show a difference of 0.5 percent between the poles and the equator.

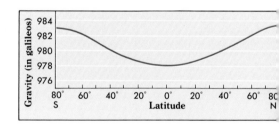

Altitude and gravity

As distance from the center of the Earth increases, gravitational force declines. On top of a mountain, or on the upper floors of a skyscraper *(below, left)*, the attractive force is less than it is at the bottom. The rate at which gravity decreases as altitude rises is constant everywhere on the planet.

Time and gravity

When the gravity at a given spot is measured over a period of time, as shown below, it is found to vary slightly. The changes follow a cycle of about 12½ hours and result from a slight bulging of the Earth; this in turn is caused by the gravitational pull of the Sun and Moon.

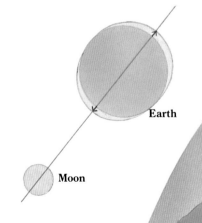

Earth

Moon

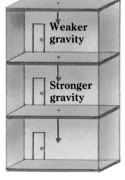

Weaker gravity

Stronger gravity

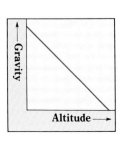

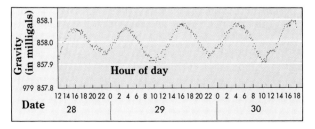

Date 28 29 30

Location and gravity

The geological formations surrounding a site can influence gravity measured at that location. Mountains, for example, alter both the strength and the direction of the gravitational pull.

To ensure accurate measurements of the gravity of a site, scientists factor in time, latitude, altitude, and nearby geological formations.

Even after they make these allowances, however, differences often remain. The anomalies result from variations in the structure and composition of the Earth below the measurement point. Dense materials increase the gravitational pull; less dense materials reduce it. Such anomalies help geologists determine the makeup of the Earth.

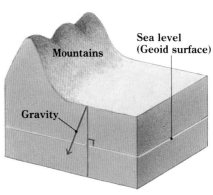

Gravitational anomalies reveal the presence of geologic structures beneath the surface. Because the mantle is denser than the crust, positive anomalies indicate a thin crust; negative anomalies show where it is thick.

Mountains and gravity

In the 19th century, British surveyors in India found that a weight suspended on a string at point C was being drawn away from its vertical position and toward the nearby Himalayas. This indicated that the enormous mass of a mountain range exerts a gravitational force of its own. But the pull of the Himalayas was less than measurements of their mass indicated it should be; this in turn gave geologists the first clues that led to the theory of isostasy *(pages 10-11)*.

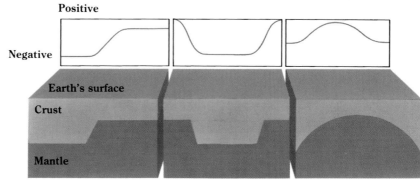

Why Does a Compass Point to North?

When a compass is held near a simple bar magnet, the north pole of the compass needle points toward the south pole of the magnet. The Earth, which is a gigantic magnet itself, makes a compass act the same way; the compass needle points toward the south pole of Earth's magnetic field, which happens to be located near the planet's North Pole.

Earth's core creates the planet's magnetic field. The fluid outer core has a high iron content and is therefore an excellent conductor of electricity. As the fluid moves in response to internal heat flows or the Earth's rotation, it generates an electric current that makes the core a huge electromagnet.

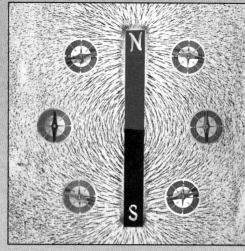

▲**Iron filings** around a bar magnet reveal lines of magnetic force. A compass needle will rest parallel to these lines.

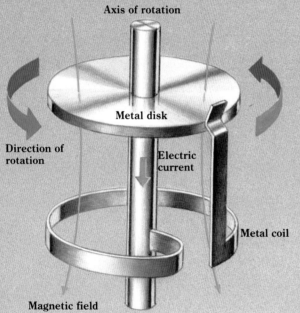

Axis of rotation

Metal disk

Direction of rotation

Electric current

Metal coil

Magnetic field

● **The Earth as dynamo**

As shown at right, Earth's outer core creates an electric current that in turn generates a magnetic field.

1 According to the dynamo theory, illustrated at left, the motion of iron-rich fluid in Earth's outer core generates both an electric current and Earth's magnetic field. The metal disk represents fluid in the outer core; when the disk rotates, it produces a current that flows downward along the axis of rotation.

2 The current flowing down the axis *(right)* returns to the disk through the metal coil. The faster the rotation, the stronger the resulting magnetic field *(blue arrows)*.

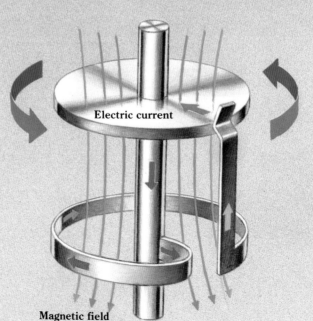

Electric current

Magnetic field

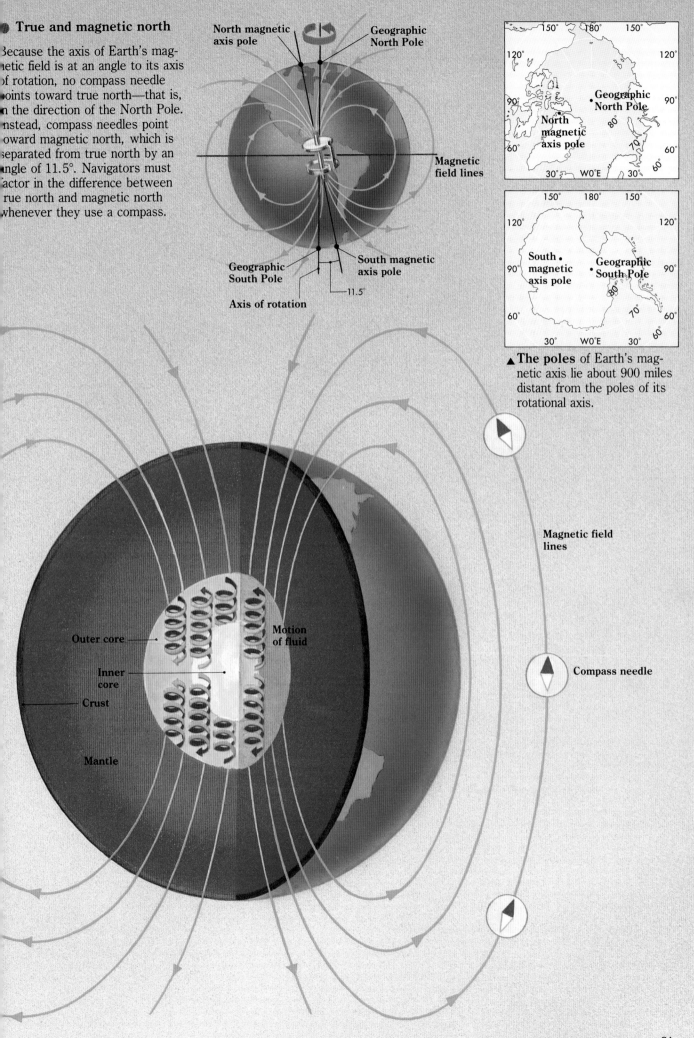

True and magnetic north

Because the axis of Earth's magnetic field is at an angle to its axis of rotation, no compass needle points toward true north—that is, in the direction of the North Pole. Instead, compass needles point toward magnetic north, which is separated from true north by an angle of 11.5°. Navigators must factor in the difference between true north and magnetic north whenever they use a compass.

North magnetic axis pole

Geographic North Pole

Magnetic field lines

Geographic South Pole

South magnetic axis pole

11.5°

Axis of rotation

▲ **The poles** of Earth's magnetic axis lie about 900 miles distant from the poles of its rotational axis.

150° 180° 150°
120° 120°
90° Geographic North Pole 90°
North magnetic axis pole 80°
60° 70° 60°
30° W0°E 30°

150° 180° 150°
120° 120°
South magnetic axis pole 90° Geographic South Pole 90°
80°
60° 70° 60°
30° W0°E 30°

Magnetic field lines

Compass needle

Outer core

Inner core

Crust

Motion of fluid

Mantle

21

2

When Continents Collide

Earth is a planet in constant flux, its surface a mass of colliding continents and shifting seas. Far from being a seamless cover, this outer layer is fractured into a dozen or so rigid plates that ride on a layer of nearly molten rock beneath. Propelled by various forces deep within the Earth, these immense rafts of stone carry the continents with them as they move.

A great deal of geologic action, marked by numerous earthquakes, takes place at the boundaries of these shifting plates. The plates crash head-on, split apart, or simply grind their edges together as they pass, giving rise to the Earth's major surface features and geologic processes. Where plates collide, the edge of one plate plunges down into the fiery mantle, and a deep ocean trench often opens up along the line of its disappearance. Where plates pull away from each other, magma wells up from below, creating features known as mid-ocean ridges and rift valleys. And where one plate muscles past another, large faults develop and earthquakes result.

This view of the processes that shape the Earth is known as plate tectonics, from the Greek word for "construction." Developed in the 1960s, the theory ranks as perhaps the greatest advance in the history of geology. With it, geologists have a framework to understand all manner of short- and long-term events, from the occurrence of earthquakes and volcanoes to the movement of continents and the birth of mountains.

The Great Rift Valley of eastern Africa, stretching some 2,500 miles from the Red Sea to Mozambique, marks a break in the continent where the African plate is splitting apart. Along this seam an ocean arm like the Red Sea may one day develop.

Are the Continents Moving?

The Earth's continents have been slowly shifting positions for millions of years, joining together and drifting apart as the plates they ride on creep around the globe. In 1912 German meteorologist Alfred Wegener argued that the continents were once fused in a supercontinent, Pangaea ("all Earth"), which began to split apart some 200 million years ago.

Wegener's theory of continental drift did not gain acceptance until the 1960s, when geologists developed an understanding of plate motions that explained how such drift could occur. Geologists now believe that the continents were in motion even before the breakup of Pangaea. Continued drift, they speculate, may someday relink the continents, forging a truly unified Earth.

──────── Ocean trench
──────── Mid-ocean ridge
          Transform fault
  ●   Hot spot
━━━▶   Continental movement
━━━▶   Seabed movement

300 million to 200 million years ago. The continents have converged to form the supercontinent Pangaea. North America and Eurasia make up Pangaea's northern segment, called Laurasia. The other continents cluster in the southern segment, Gondwana. To the east is the Tethys Sea.

50 million years from now. The Atlantic continues to widen as the Pacific shrinks. Australia nears Asia. California west of the San Andreas fault moves north. Africa's Rift Valley opens and floods. The Red Sea widens, and the Persian Gulf disappears.

5

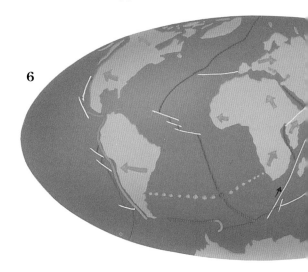

6

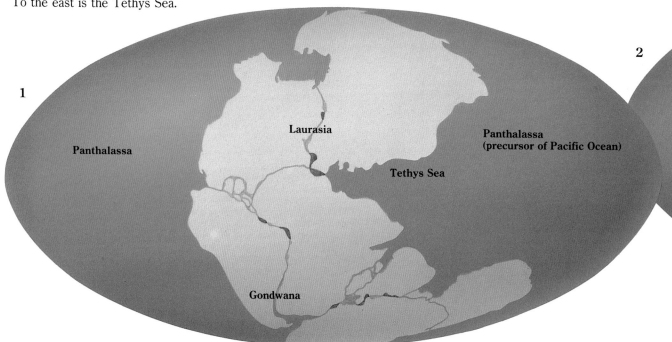

1

2

Laurasia

Panthalassa

Panthalassa
(precursor of Pacific Ocean)

Tethys Sea

Gondwana

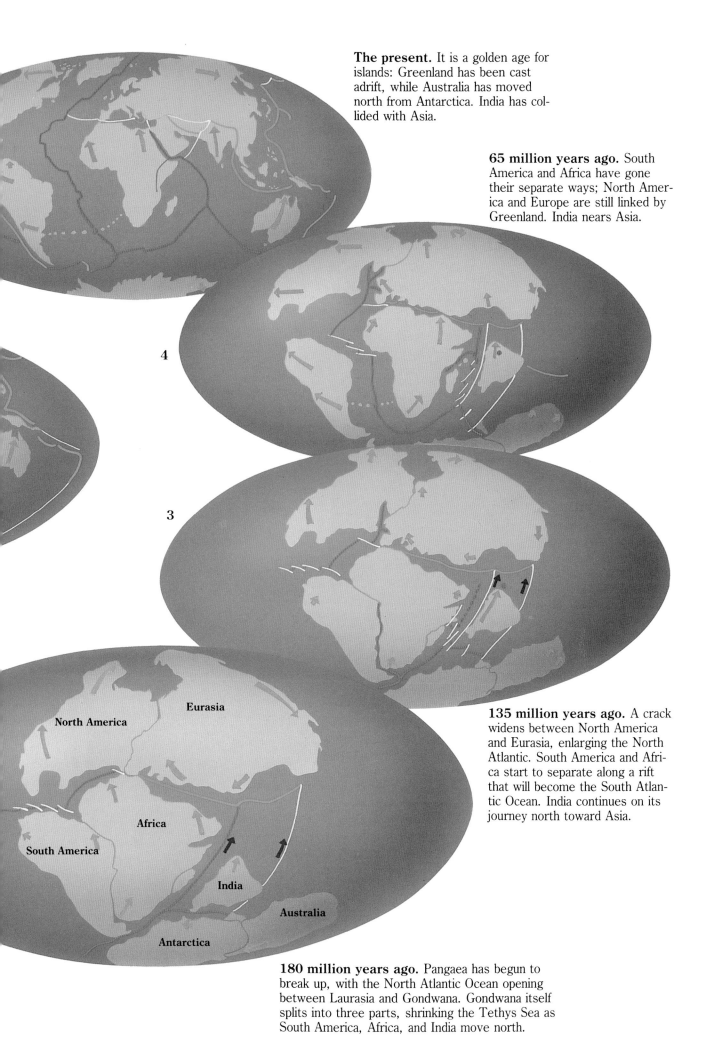

The present. It is a golden age for islands: Greenland has been cast adrift, while Australia has moved north from Antarctica. India has collided with Asia.

65 million years ago. South America and Africa have gone their separate ways; North America and Europe are still linked by Greenland. India nears Asia.

4

3

Eurasia

North America

Africa

South America

India

Australia

Antarctica

135 million years ago. A crack widens between North America and Eurasia, enlarging the North Atlantic. South America and Africa start to separate along a rift that will become the South Atlantic Ocean. India continues on its journey north toward Asia.

180 million years ago. Pangaea has begun to break up, with the North Atlantic Ocean opening between Laurasia and Gondwana. Gondwana itself splits into three parts, shrinking the Tethys Sea as South America, Africa, and India move north.

Is There Proof of Continental Drift?

Many bits of evidence support the belief that the continents once belonged to a single giant land-mass that later broke up and drifted apart. The most obvious clue is the near-perfect match made by the coastlines of distant continents, such as South America and Africa, suggesting that these landmasses were once interlocked. Another piece of evidence lies in fossils: Identical remains of certain plant and animal species have been found on continents that today are separated by oceans. Mineral evidence, too—coal deposits in Antarctica, for example—shows the continents have experienced climates that could not have occurred at their present locations.

Added proof of continental drift comes from related rock formations beside the Atlantic Ocean; these drop off at one coast only to reappear in identical form on the opposite shore. Sev-

Modern Earth

Present-day equator

South Pole

Ancient equator

Africa

India

South America

Australia

Earth 300 million years ago

An icy diaspora

About 300 million years ago, glaciers *(shaded white at left)* covered the tips of the southern continents. One explanation for this fact is the theory that the areas were joined near the South Pole.

Transatlantic snails

The common garden snail lives on both sides of the Atlantic, a body of water it could not have crossed on its own. Geologists believe that these distant habitats, shown in red at left, once lay side by side.

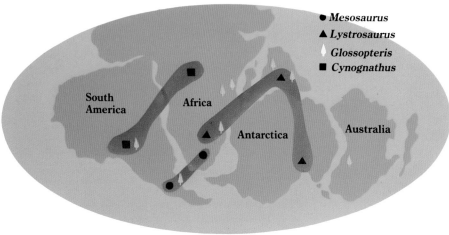

- ● *Mesosaurus*
- ▲ *Lystrosaurus*
- ◊ *Glossopteris*
- ■ *Cynognathus*

South America

Africa

Antarctica

Australia

Far-fetched fossils

As shown at left, fossils of the fernlike *Glossopteris* and the reptiles *Lystrosaurus, Mesosaurus,* and *Cynognathus*—all of which lived more than 200 million years ago—are scattered across several continents, a sign that the continents were once joined. Today's oceans would have kept these land dwellers from migrating.

eral continents also have similar glacial deposits.

The most convincing evidence has an unusual source. Studies of the alignment of magnetic particles in ancient rocks show that the continents have moved since the rocks first formed.

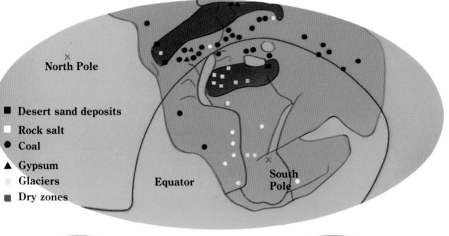

Desert sand deposits
Rock salt
Coal
Gypsum
Glaciers
Dry zones

North Pole

Equator

South Pole

Clues from ancient climes

Evidence of ancient coral reefs and desert sand dunes, as well as deposits of coal, salt, and gypsum, turns up in many places where today's climate would not allow them to form. These sites make sense if the continents are shifted to their former positions, as shown at left.

North America

Europe

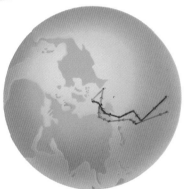

Peregrinating poles

The magnetic properties of ancient rocks reveal that Earth's magnetic poles have migrated over time. North American rocks suggest a different migratory path than European rocks *(far left)*. Only if the continents were once joined do the two paths correspond *(left)*.

le migration for Europe *(red)* and North merica *(blue)* assuming fixed continents

Pole migration for Europe *(red)* and North America *(blue)* assuming continental drift

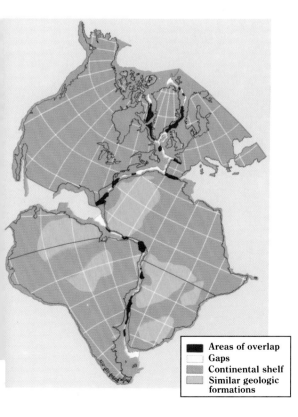

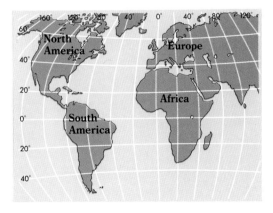

North America

Europe

Africa

South America

Areas of overlap
Gaps
Continental shelf
Similar geologic formations

A giant jigsaw

An accurate world map like the one above can be manipulated by computer to restore the continents to their original positions *(left)*. Africa and South America—including their continental shelves—fit together snugly. When similar geologic features *(orange)* are factored in, the continents match in rock type and structure as well as in contour.

What Makes the Earth's Surface Move?

Heat inside the Earth is the driving force behind plate tectonics, the processes that cause seafloors to spread and continents to move. As this heat rises through the mantle, it deforms the lithosphere—the brittle skin of rock that composes the planet's rigid outer layer—and breaks it into large plates. These plates, each about 60 miles thick, move slowly but steadily over the asthenosphere, the layer of upper-mantle rock that is so hot it yields and flows like molten plastic.

When two plates move apart, molten rock rises from the asthenosphere to fill the gap, creating new lithosphere. When two plates collide, the edge of one plunges under the other and into the asthenosphere, where it is consumed by the mantle's high heat; this is known as subduction.

Geologists theorize that heat motions called convection currents power the movement of the plates; according to this view, the Earth's high internal heat mixes the mantle material like a simmering pot of oatmeal. But scientists disagree about just how the plates move. Some believe that the plates ride passively on rising and descending columns of heat. Others contend that the plates actively help propel themselves; according to this view, the weight of the sinking edge of a plate pulls the rest of the plate down toward the subduction zone.

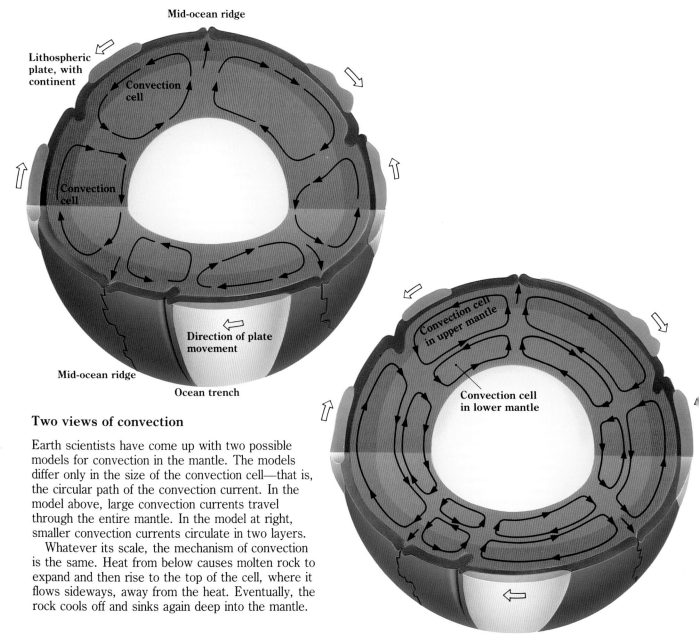

Two views of convection

Earth scientists have come up with two possible models for convection in the mantle. The models differ only in the size of the convection cell—that is, the circular path of the convection current. In the model above, large convection currents travel through the entire mantle. In the model at right, smaller convection currents circulate in two layers.

Whatever its scale, the mechanism of convection is the same. Heat from below causes molten rock to expand and then rise to the top of the cell, where it flows sideways, away from the heat. Eventually, the rock cools off and sinks again deep into the mantle.

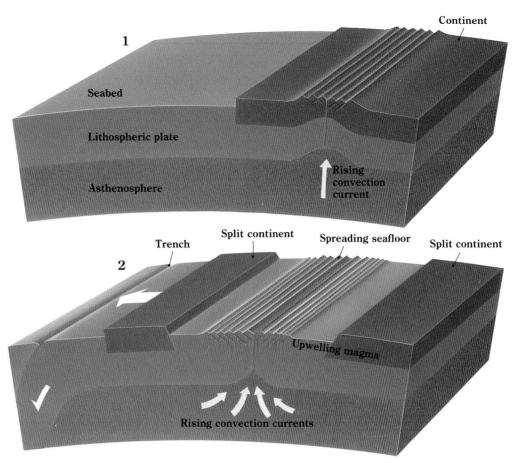

wo lands from one

s shown in Step 1 at right,
sing convective heat cur-
nts *(yellow arrow)* begin
e process of splitting a
ntinent. First, the heat
uses the continental crust
arch upward in a dome;
er millions of years, the
me stretches to the
eaking point. The crustal
ates then split, a rift val-
y forms, and the ocean
arts to invade. As the
ates continue to diverge,
welling magma forms a
id-ocean ridge (Step 2).

The pull of a subducted plate

The three-step diagram at left illus-
trates the "active" theory of subduction, a collision in which one crustal
plate overrides another. According to
this view, the lithosphere functions as
the top of the convection cell, and
lithospheric plates actively pull themselves along. As the new lithosphere
moves away from the mid-ocean ridge
where it formed, it cools, thickens, and
becomes more dense, causing it to lose
buoyancy and sink deeper into the asthenosphere (Steps 1 and 2). When
enough of the plate edge has sunk, its
weight drags the rest of the plate after
it (Step 3), following the downward leg
of the convection current. The active
theory thus argues that plates move
independently of the mantle beneath,
and that they may even help drive the
mantle's convective processes.

Has Seafloor Spreading Been Proved?

The bottom of the sea was a little-known realm until the 1950s, when recently developed technologies such as sonar enabled geographers to map the ocean floor. These maps revealed a startling feature that helped explain continental drift: A system of oceanic ridges was found rising high above the seafloor, forming a submarine mountain chain that winds some 52,000 miles through all the world's oceans.

Along the crest of the oceanic ridges runs a deep valley, called a rift valley, where magma from the mantle wells up to the surface, creating new seafloor in a process called seafloor spreading. As new rock is added in the rift valley, the rocks to either side are gradually pushed away from the center of the ridge, as if on twin conveyor belts. Thus the seafloor increases in age with increasing distance from the ridge.

Proof that the ocean floor is spreading lies in the magnetic orientation of seabed rocks. When rocks form in the rift valley, they become magnetized in the direction of Earth's existing magnetic field, which has reversed its orientation countless times through history. This magnetic flip-flopping is why alternately magnetized bands of rock parallel most ocean ridges: As each new batch of rock cools down and moves aside, it assumes the orientation of Earth's magnetic field at that time.

Further proof comes from ocean sediments; their thickness and age increase with distance from the ridge, revealing the increasing age of the seafloor beneath them.

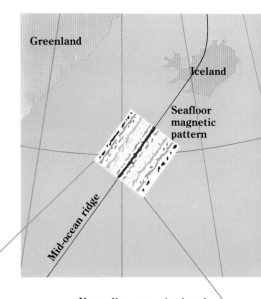

A record of reversals

The seafloor on both sides of the Mid-Atlantic Ridge south of Iceland has bands of alternating magnetism that match the history of Earth's magnetic reversals. As the seafloor spreads out from the ridge, each new band of rock splits down the middle, forming a mirror image.

Young at fault

The record of magnetic reversals on the ocean floor matches that found in continental rocks, the ages of which have been determined by isotopic dating. The seafloor's magnetic patterns can therefore be used to prepare a map *(right)* that shows the seafloor's age. Such age-coded maps confirm that the youngest seafloor parallels the mid-ocean ridges and that the oldest seafloor abuts continental shelves or ocean trenches. With the seafloor spreading at an average of ½ inch to 2 inches per year, virtually no part of the ocean bottom is more than 200 million years old.

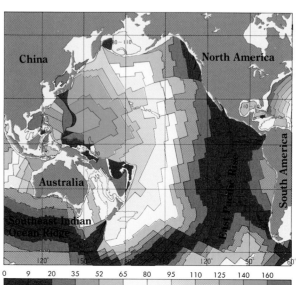

| 0 | 9 | 20 | 35 | 52 | 65 | 80 | 95 | 110 | 125 | 140 | 160 | Age in millions of years |

Measuring drift with a quasar

A technique called VLBI (Very Long Baseline Interferometry) gauges the rate of seafloor spreading and continental drift. The secret of VLBI's success is its ability to precisely measure the distance between two faraway points—that is, the ends of a very long baseline.

As shown at right and below, paired VLBI antennas pick up radio waves from a quasar, a tiny but extraordinarily bright galaxy. Computers then calculate the difference in the time it took a given wave to reach the two points. This time difference changes as the points move closer together or farther apart, so a year-to-year comparison reveals the pace at which the ground stations are nearing or receding from each other. In 1989 Hawaii drifted a quarter-inch closer to Japan.

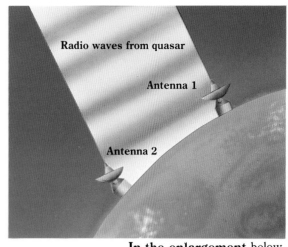

Radio waves from quasar

Antenna 1

Antenna 2

In the enlargement below, an oceanographic vessel uses a drill to extract core samples from the seabed. The samples can then be dated.

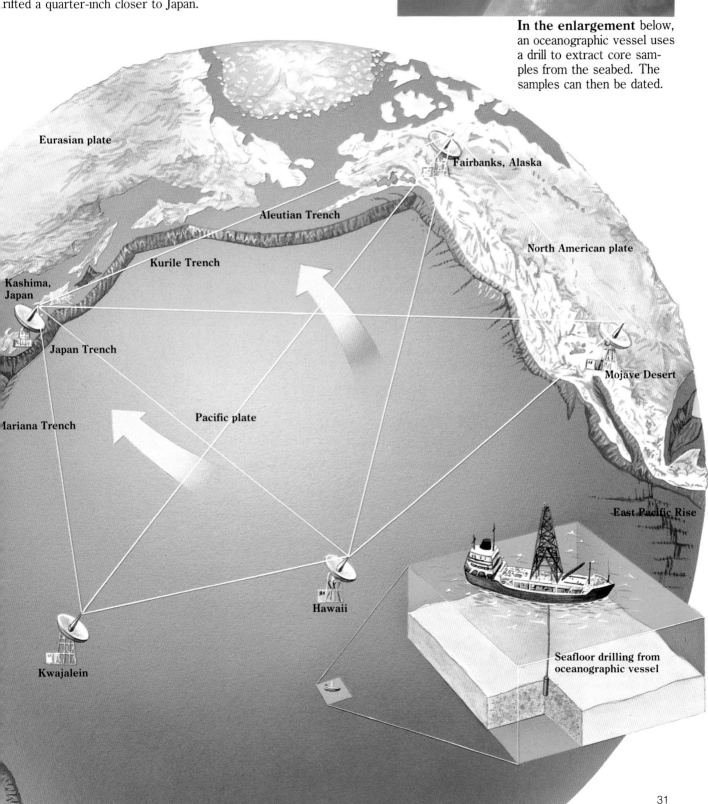

Eurasian plate

Fairbanks, Alaska

Aleutian Trench

North American plate

Kurile Trench

Kashima, Japan

Japan Trench

Mojave Desert

Mariana Trench

Pacific plate

East Pacific Rise

Hawaii

Seafloor drilling from oceanographic vessel

Kwajalein

How Is New Ocean Floor Made?

Mid-ocean ridges, dividing lines between crustal plates, are hotbeds of volcanism. In the last 200 million years or so, these factories of stone have been responsible for regenerating more than 50 percent of the Earth's lithosphere.

Most of this volcanic activity is quiet and gradual rather than explosive. A heat current rising through the mantle warms a section of ocean crust, expanding and thinning it. Eventually, the crust fractures. Enormous chunks of crust subside, forming a rift valley up to a mile deep and 20 miles wide. Magma then oozes upward through fissures, or underground cracks; if it gets to the surface, it may spread over the rift floor or it may solidify beneath the rift zone. The fissuring and volcanism continue in a cycle, constantly creating new lithosphere.

The new ocean crust inches outward on both sides of the rift zone, cooling off as it goes. In this way, rock forged on ridges 2 miles above the seabed ultimately becomes part of the great plain covering the ocean floor.

Building a seafloor, layer by layer

Three types of volcanism in the rift zone yield a layered crust. Where faulting opens fissures, magma seeps to the surface, forming a bulbous, lumpy mass known as pillow lava. Alternatively, the magma may congeal within the fissures, producing vertical sheetlike dikes. Some magma never reaches the surface; instead, it slowly crystallizes in the lower crust into a rock called gabbro. Ocean sediments gradually add a final layer on top of this igneous crust.

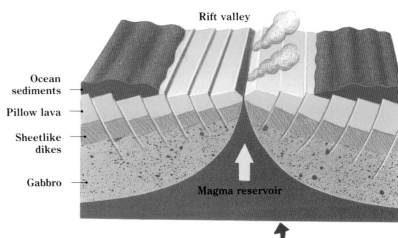

Rift valley
Ocean sediments
Pillow lava
Sheetlike dikes
Gabbro
Magma reservoir

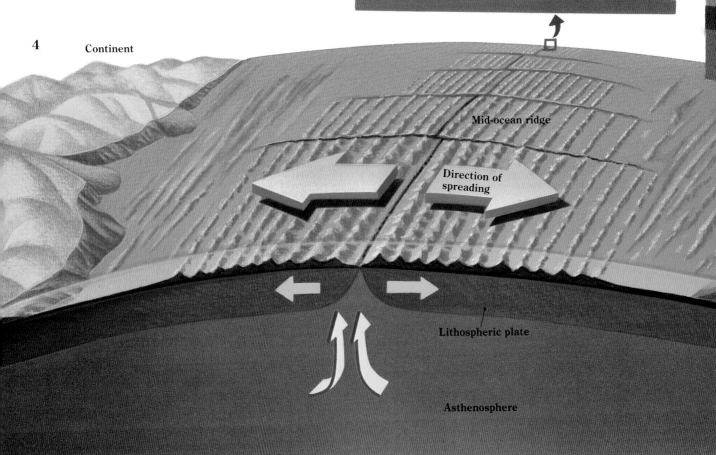

4

Continent

Mid-ocean ridge

Direction of spreading

Lithospheric plate

Asthenosphere

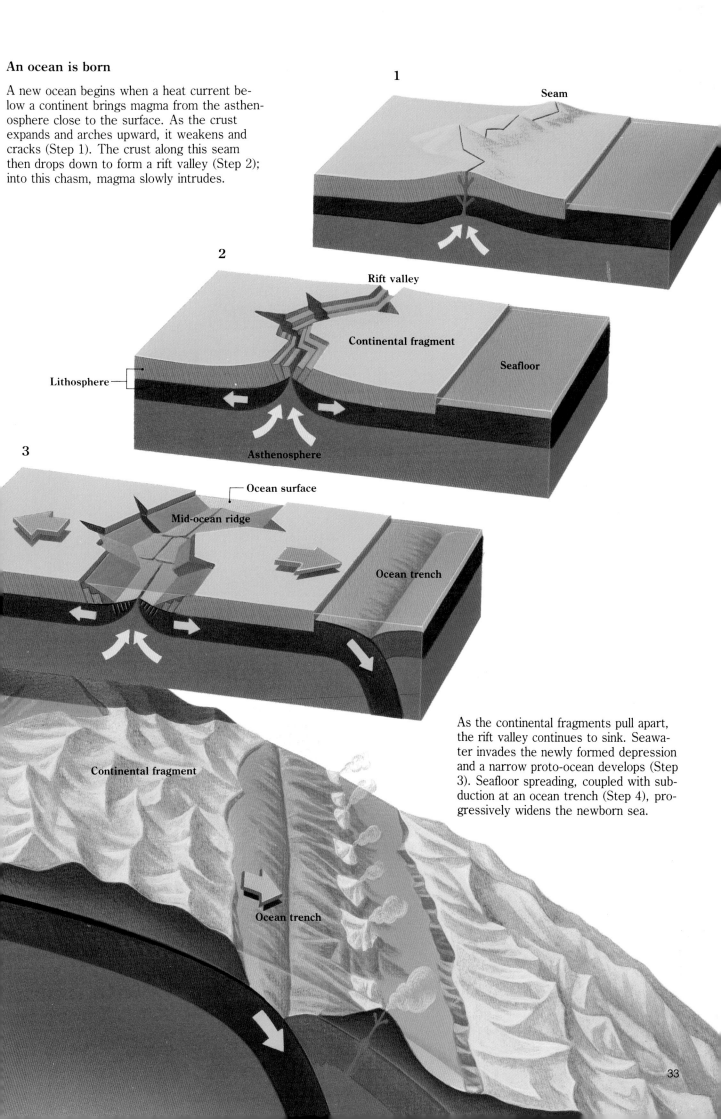

An ocean is born

A new ocean begins when a heat current below a continent brings magma from the asthenosphere close to the surface. As the crust expands and arches upward, it weakens and cracks (Step 1). The crust along this seam then drops down to form a rift valley (Step 2); into this chasm, magma slowly intrudes.

1

Seam

2

Rift valley

Continental fragment

Seafloor

Lithosphere

Asthenosphere

3

Ocean surface

Mid-ocean ridge

Ocean trench

Continental fragment

Ocean trench

As the continental fragments pull apart, the rift valley continues to sink. Seawater invades the newly formed depression and a narrow proto-ocean develops (Step 3). Seafloor spreading, coupled with subduction at an ocean trench (Step 4), progressively widens the newborn sea.

Are All Plate Boundaries the Same?

Three types of borders separate Earth's tectonic plates. A divergent boundary marks the line where two plates move apart. Examples of divergent boundaries include oceanic ridges and Africa's Great Rift Valley. A convergent boundary, by contrast, is formed at the site where two plates collide. If one or both plates are part of the ocean floor, the collision results in a deep-sea trench. If both plates hold continents, the continental margins collide, crumple, and lift up into a mountain range. A convergent boundary exists at the edge of the Himalayas. Finally, a transform or shear boundary demarcates the meeting points of two plates that grind past each other. The intense friction generated during this plate side-swiping causes earthquakes to occur along fractures known as transform faults. The best-known example of a transform boundary is the San Andreas fault.

The Icelandic rift valley shown above follows an exposed portion of the Mid-Atlantic Ridge, the divergent boundary between two oceanic plates.

Three types of plate borders

A divergent boundary

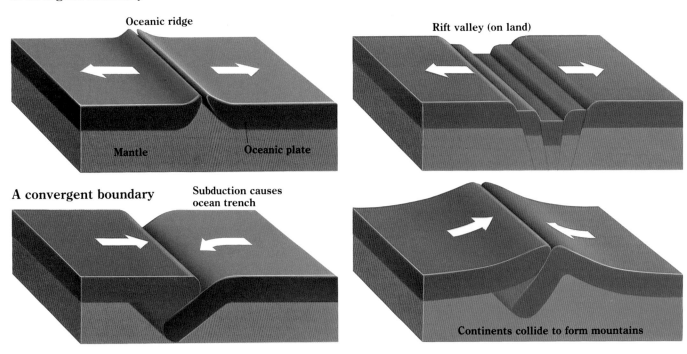

Oceanic ridge

Mantle   Oceanic plate

Rift valley (on land)

A convergent boundary   Subduction causes ocean trench

Continents collide to form mountains

A transform boundary

Transform fault

When the edge of one plate grinds against the edge of a second plate moving in the opposite direction, a transform fault results.

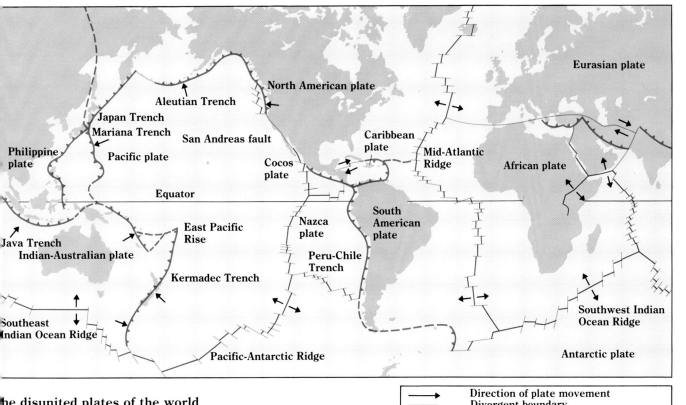

The disunited plates of the world

The boundaries of Earth's major tectonic plates are shown above. Most plate margins are geologically active—that is, earthquakes or volcanoes are much more frequent along these borders than anywhere else. Some plates are covered almost entirely by ocean crust; others provide the foundation for large areas of continental crust. The rate of plate movement varies widely, from almost no movement in Africa to 4 inches per year in parts of the Pacific.

What's in a plate boundary?

Cut in half along the equator *(red line, right)*, the Earth reveals the plate boundaries of the eastern Pacific *(below)*. An oceanic ridge, its course staggered by transform faults, forms the divergent boundary between the Pacific plate to the west and the Nazca plate to the east. As the Pacific plate moves northwest, it will eventually slide into deep-sea trenches off the coast of Alaska and Eurasia. The Nazca plate, meanwhile, will someday dive below the South American plate in the Peru-Chile Trench.

→	Direction of plate movement
	Divergent boundary
	Transform fault
▲▲▲	Convergent boundary
- - -	Uncharted boundary

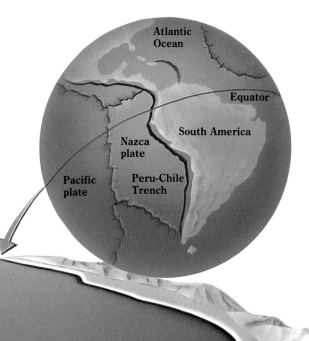

What Happens When Continents Collide?

The type of rock that makes up continental crust is lighter than the rock beneath the ocean floor; when two such plates collide, therefore, the ocean crust is subducted beneath the more buoyant continental crust. When the plates involved in a collision both carry continents, however, their equal buoyancy prevents either landmass from sinking very deep into the mantle. As the continents ram together, their margins are welded, compressed, and uplifted into mountain ranges. These titanic clashes often yield spectacular scenery; the Himalayas *(right)* and the Alps are prime examples.

Tall and still growing, the Himalayan peaks rise about 2 inches higher each year as the Indian plate continues its slow advance beneath Asia.

A simply smashing start

After the breakup of Pangaea, India became an island continent, sailing north toward Asia. About 50 million years ago, near present-day Tibet, a trench swallowed the oceanic leading edge of the Indian plate; the mantle melted the plate's leading edge, and the resulting magma rose up through volcanoes along the Asian coast (Step 1). Then, as the continental crust of India slammed into Asia (Step 2), sediments from the sea that had separated the two continents were crushed and folded between them; mountain building began. India continued to press forward, wedging its way beneath the Asian crust (Step 3) and raising the Himalayas to towering heights.

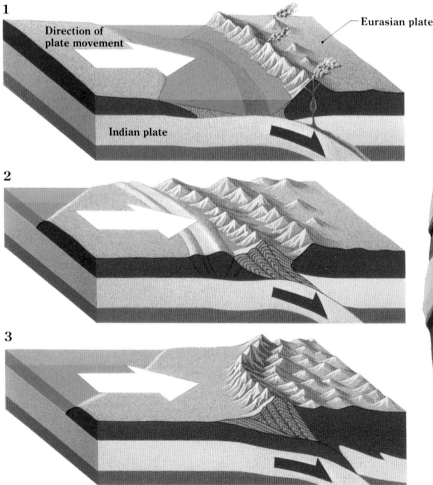

1

Direction of plate movement

Eurasian plate

Indian plate

2

3

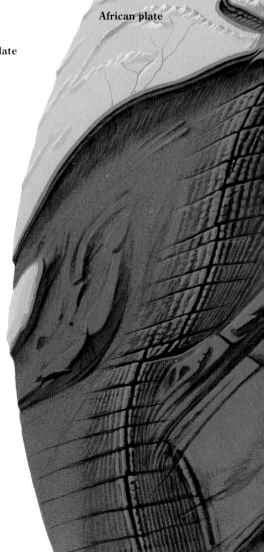

African plate

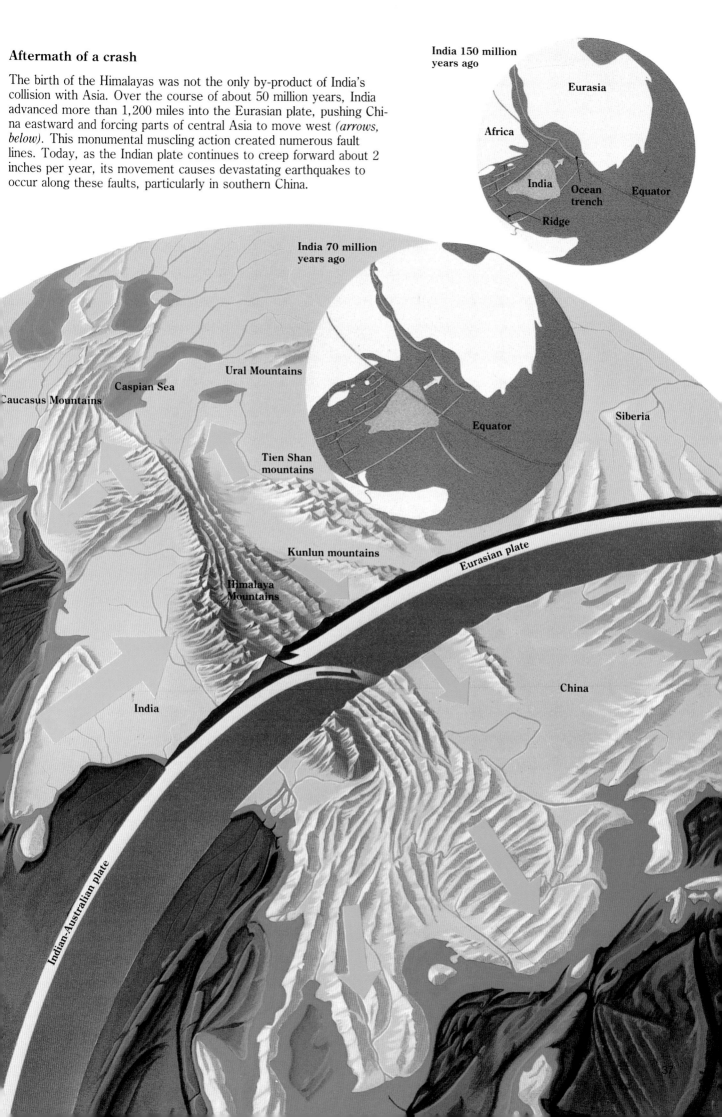

Aftermath of a crash

The birth of the Himalayas was not the only by-product of India's collision with Asia. Over the course of about 50 million years, India advanced more than 1,200 miles into the Eurasian plate, pushing China eastward and forcing parts of central Asia to move west *(arrows, below)*. This monumental muscling action created numerous fault lines. Today, as the Indian plate continues to creep forward about 2 inches per year, its movement causes devastating earthquakes to occur along these faults, particularly in southern China.

India 150 million years ago

Eurasia

Africa

India

Ocean trench

Equator

Ridge

India 70 million years ago

Ural Mountains

Caspian Sea

Caucasus Mountains

Equator

Siberia

Tien Shan mountains

Eurasian plate

Kunlun mountains

Himalaya Mountains

China

India

Indian-Australian plate

How Did the Andes Mountains Form?

When the Nazca plate plunged beneath South America in the trench along that continent's western edge, it did not melt quietly back into the asthenosphere. Instead, the sinking plate crumpled the edge of the continent into a folded and faulted mountain belt. Then, as the leading edge of the plate reached the superheated mantle and began to melt, magma bubbled up through the continental crust and erupted in numerous volcanoes. Some less dense magma remained in a huge reservoir within the crust; as this molten rock rose and slowly solidified, it lifted and deformed the rock above it. Together these forces created the Andes mountains.

200 million years ago

South America was still part of Pangaea, the conglomerate landmass in which all of today's continents were once fused together.

140 million years ago

South America and Africa had split apart; the South American plate was beginning to drift west. As the continent slid over the Nazca plate, its west edge crumpled into folded mountains. Volcanoes, fed by magma from the sinking plate, formed offshore.

65 million years ago

The Nazca plate had continued to be drawn downward; the resulting volcanoes had added material to the continental crust. Below the surface, a giant pool of magma had congealed to form the basement rock of the Andes, arching the crust upward.

Pacific Ocean

South Americ

South America

Mid-Atlantic Ridge

Pacific plate

Upwelling magma in East Pacific Rise

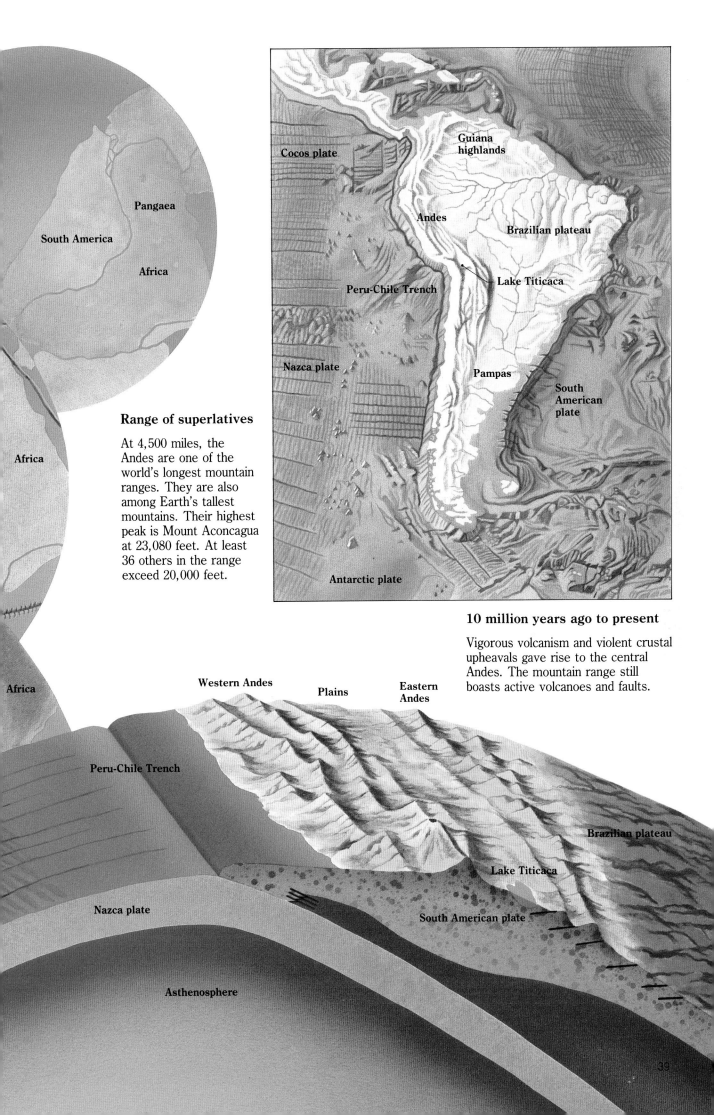

Pangaea

South America

Africa

Africa

Africa

Cocos plate

Guiana highlands

Andes

Brazilian plateau

Lake Titicaca

Peru-Chile Trench

Nazca plate

Pampas

South American plate

Antarctic plate

Range of superlatives

At 4,500 miles, the Andes are one of the world's longest mountain ranges. They are also among Earth's tallest mountains. Their highest peak is Mount Aconcagua at 23,080 feet. At least 36 others in the range exceed 20,000 feet.

10 million years ago to present

Vigorous volcanism and violent crustal upheavals gave rise to the central Andes. The mountain range still boasts active volcanoes and faults.

Western Andes

Plains

Eastern Andes

Peru-Chile Trench

Brazilian plateau

Lake Titicaca

Nazca plate

South American plate

Asthenosphere

How Was the Great Rift Valley Made?

The same forces that created the world's mid-ocean ridges also formed the Great Rift Valley of Africa. This impressive cleft—actually a string of sunken valleys and lake basins that pockmark the landscape for 2,500 miles from Ethiopia to Mozambique—represents an early stage in the rupture of the African plate.

Starting about 15 million years ago, an upsurge of magma from the mantle swelled East Africa's crust into a dome. The crust along the top of this rise stretched and then subsided, or collapsed in long troughs, to form the present rift zone. Volcanoes along the rift have sculpted such landmarks as 19,340-foot-high Mount Kilimanjaro and 17,058-foot-high Mount Kenya.

The steep walls of Africa's Great Rift Valley bear witness to the dramatic faulting that dropped this swath of crust thousands of feet below the Ethiopian plateau.

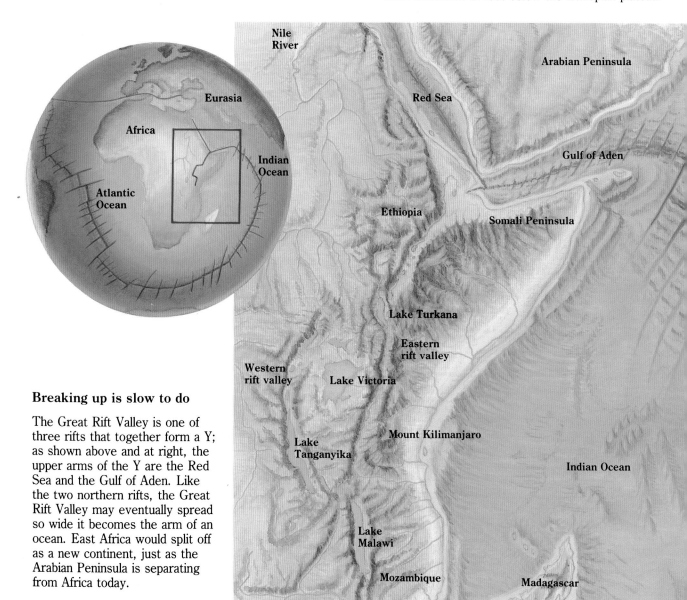

Breaking up is slow to do

The Great Rift Valley is one of three rifts that together form a Y; as shown above and at right, the upper arms of the Y are the Red Sea and the Gulf of Aden. Like the two northern rifts, the Great Rift Valley may eventually spread so wide it becomes the arm of an ocean. East Africa would split off as a new continent, just as the Arabian Peninsula is separating from Africa today.

Evolution of a rift valley

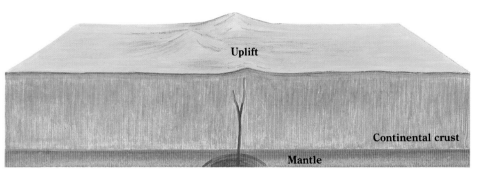

First upheaval

Hot magma produced by the mantle rises through the crust. As a result, the surface of the ground expands and arches upward.

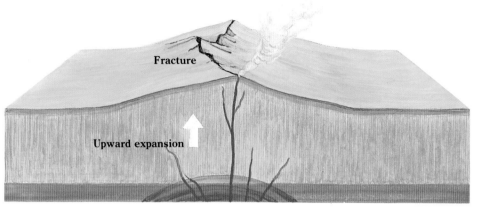

Dome formation

Magma continues to well up, raising the crust into a dome; over millions of years, the dome stretches and weakens until it fractures.

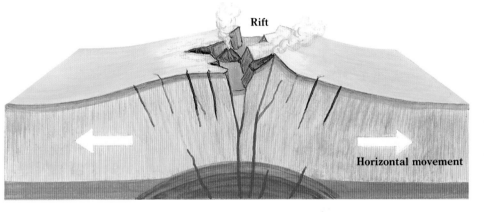

Rift and separate

As the crust pulls apart, faults open and blocks of crust subside, letting volcanoes erupt. The Great Rift Valley is currently at this stage.

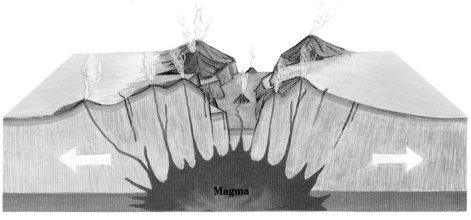

Volcanism on the rise

The fissures multiply, providing numerous additional outlets for the magma. Volcanic activity intensifies in and along the rift. The northern Red Sea typifies this stage of rifting.

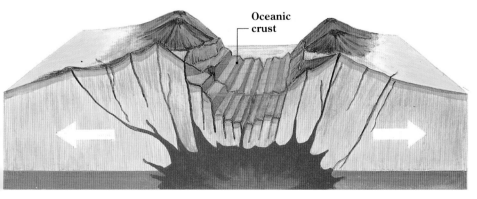

The final split

The rift sinks as it widens, allowing the sea to invade. The rising magma creates a finger of oceanic crust, and seafloor spreading begins. The southern Red Sea and the Gulf of Aden are at this stage.

What Is the San Andreas Fault?

Zigzagging 800 miles through densely populated regions of coastal California, the San Andreas fault is one of the most notorious transform faults in the world. It delineates a transform boundary where the Pacific plate, carrying a small sliver of continental crust, grinds past the North American plate. The result of this movement is frequent earthquakes.

A fault has not always occupied the site. Before the San Andreas was formed, an ocean trench lay here, swallowing up an ancient plate,

called the Farallon plate, that was sandwiched between the Pacific and North American plates. Westward movement of the North American plate over the Farallon plate eventually consumed it at the trench boundary. Then, as the westward-moving North American plate met the Pacific plate, subduction at the trench ceased. The North American plate overrode the East Pacific Rise and its transform faults, and one of those faults cut the North American plate to become the San Andreas fault.

Tearing the terrain in two, the San Andreas fault winds north-south through California. Land west of the fault rides on the Pacific plate, which is moving northwest about 2 inches per year. In some areas of the fault, the plates' jagged edges lock together; the crustal rocks are strained until they lurch forward to a new position, radiating shock waves—an earthquake—from the point of rupture.

From trench to fault

The diagrams below show how the convergent boundary, or trench, that once existed off the North American coast changed to a transform fault.

40 million years ago

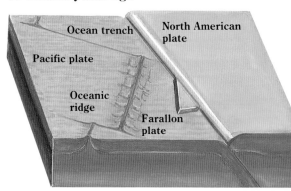

25 million years ago

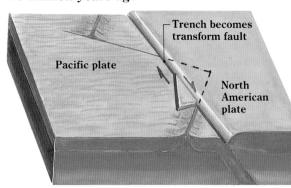

Present day

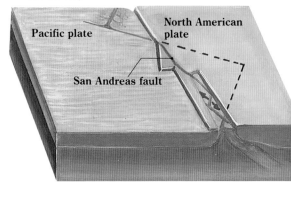

The birth of a fault

Some 40 million years ago, the Farallon plate was being subducted, or gobbled up, in a trench off the California coast *(below, left)*. Over time, the northern end of the oceanic ridge separating the Farallon and Pacific plates reached the trench; the ridge itself then began to be subducted. Where the ridge was consumed, the trench became a transform fault.

As more of the ridge was subducted, the fault spread south. By about 25 million years ago, the entire ridge had been swal-lowed and the fault had reached the Gulf of California—which, in turn, began to widen as the overridden ridge continued to spread *(below, center)*.

Unlike most transform faults, which run short distances through the ocean, the San Andreas traces a lengthy course on land. (For this reason, it is often termed a strike-slip fault.) Like other transform faults, however, the San Andreas does connect segments of two mid-ocean ridges: the East Pacific Rise and the Gorda Ridge *(below, right)*.

40 million years ago

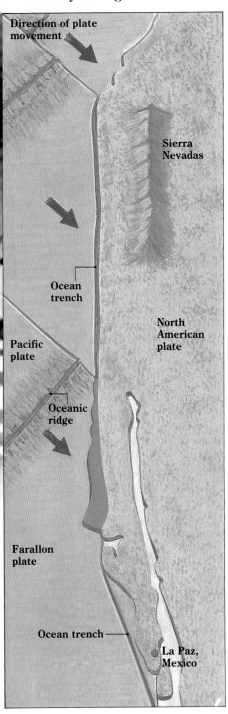

25 million years ago

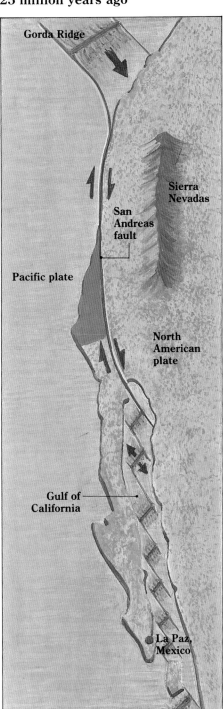

Present day

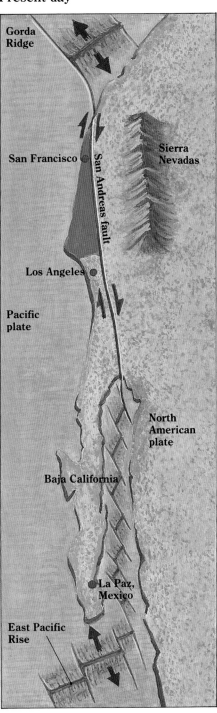

43

How Did Hawaii Come to Be?

Islands young and old

The Hawaiian Islands and the Emperor seamounts form a 3,700-mile-long chain that increases in age from one end to the other. The youngest member, the island of Hawaii, is less than a million years old. The oldest—a submarine island, or seamount, near the Aleutian Trench—formed 70 million years ago.

Aleutian Trench

Suiko seamount
(60 million years old)

Ojin seamount
(50 million years old)

Emperor seamounts

Kammu seamount
(40 million years old)

Midway (16 million years old)

Laysan

Necker (10 million years old)

Not all of Earth's volcanic activity occurs at plate margins. Occasionally, a narrow plume of magma burns through the crust like a blowtorch, creating volcanic centers such as the Hawaiian Islands, which sit near the middle of the Pacific plate. Dubbed a hot spot, the mantle plume remains stationary while the plate above it moves.

The plate's progressive drift over the hot spot produces a chain of volcanoes, some of which rise high enough to emerge from the sea as islands. The Hawaiian chain came into being just this way, as did the Emperor seamounts—a line of submerged volcanic peaks that stretches north from the western end of the Hawaiian chain. Today, only the island of Hawaii, poised directly over the hot spot, harbors active volcanoes.

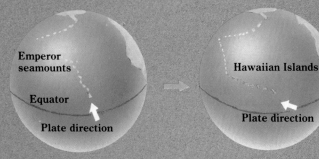

Emperor
seamounts

Equator

Plate direction

Hawaiian Islands

Plate direction

A dogleg in the sea

The Emperor seamounts lie in a straight line headed north, reflecting the northward movement of the Pacific plate at the time they formed *(left globe).*

Some 40 million years ago, the plate veered to its present northwesterly course, and the Hawaiian Islands formed along a new line *(right globe).*

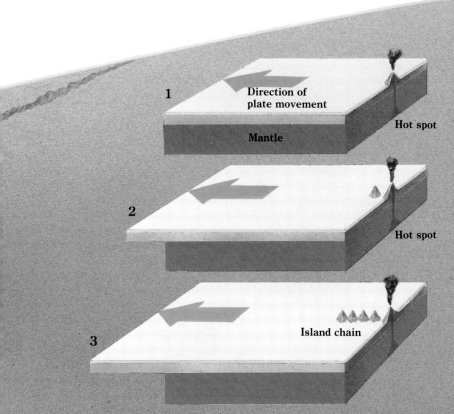

1

Direction of plate movement

Mantle

Hot spot

2

Hot spot

3

Island chain

Hot spots and island chains

An island chain starts out as a volcano above a hot spot (Step 1). The plate then drifts away from the plume; the volcano dies out, and a second volcano rises in its place (Step 2). The process recurs, yielding a chain of similar islands (Step 3). As these islands move away from the heat source, they subside and eventually become submerged.

Extinct volcanic cones pock the crater floor of Haleakala, an inactive volcano on the island of Maui.

A lava dome rises near Kilauea, the world's largest active volcano, proving that Hawaii perches on a hot spot.

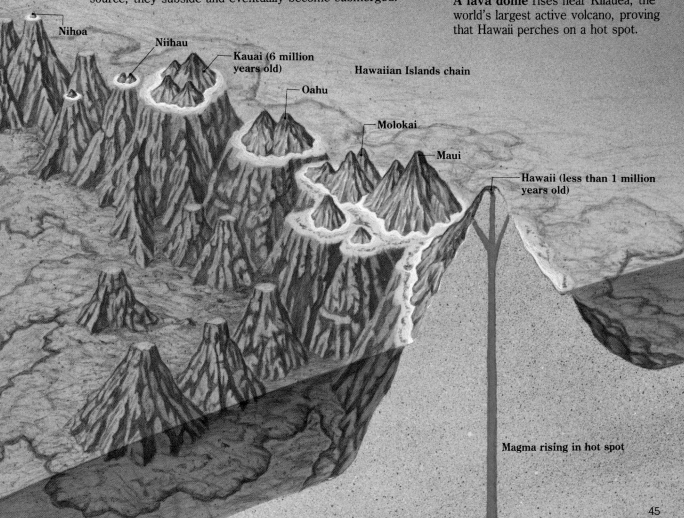

Nihoa

Niihau

Kauai (6 million years old)

Oahu

Molokai

Maui

Hawaiian Islands chain

Hawaii (less than 1 million years old)

Magma rising in hot spot

45

3
Earthquakes: Movers and Shakers

Few natural events wreak such massive destruction as earthquakes. Usually striking without warning, severe quakes generate violent vibrations that not only shake the ground but sometimes crack it open. The results can be devastating. The cataclysm that jolted the northern Chinese city of Tangshan in July 1976, for example, claimed 242,000 lives, making it the deadliest quake in two centuries.

Earthquakes large and small have racked the planet for billions of years, but their causes remained a mystery until the 1960s. During that decade, seismologists plotted thousands of earthquake epicenters and found that they cluster along well-defined belts. These belts mark the boundaries where the planet's crustal plates move relative to each other. The slow but constant movement subjects the plate borders to tremendous stress, which builds in the bedrock for decades or centuries until it is suddenly released as the vibrations, or seismic waves, that make up an earthquake. Precisely how this phenomenon occurs is the focus of this chapter.

Rescue workers in Mexico City search the rubble of buildings destroyed by an earthquake on September 19, 1985. The deadly shock, which leveled more than 400 buildings, killed some 7,000 people.

Why Do Earthquakes Occur?

Earth's outer layer is composed of huge, rocky plates that creep slowly across the globe at speeds of up to 4 inches per year. Known as tectonic plates, some of these giants carry the continents, others the ocean floors, and some a combination of the two.

Most earthquakes take place along the boundary between two plates. Propelled by heat-driven currents in the asthenosphere—that is, the softer rock beneath them—the plates constantly pull apart, collide, or grind against each other. When the strain produced by these movements increases beyond a certain level, the pent-up energy ruptures the rocks and creates a fracture known as a fault. This sudden release of energy also unleashes the ground-shaking vibrations that constitute an earthquake.

Teetering on the brink of total destruction, half a house remains after an earthquake caused the ground beneath it to subside.

A reverse fault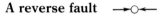

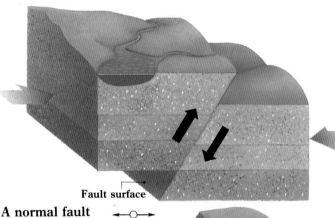

Fault surface

A normal fault

Quakes of all kinds

Plate movements produce three distinct kinds of faults. Where two plates collide *(left, top diagram)*, one side of the fracture rides up onto the other. This is called a reverse fault. Where two plates are moving apart *(left, middle diagram)*, one mass of rock moves down along the plane of the fault. Faults of this type are called normal faults. And where two plates slide past each other laterally *(left, bottom diagram)*, the fault is called a strike-slip fault.

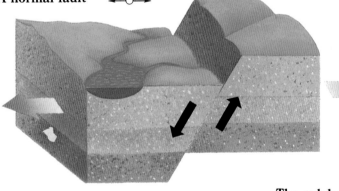

A strike-slip fault

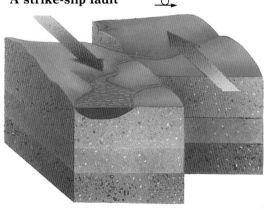

The subduction of a plate

When a plate carrying oceanic crust collides with another oceanic plate or smashes into a continental plate *(right)*, one of the two plates rides over the other, bending it steeply downward in a process known as subduction. Under great stress, the subducted plate grinds into the asthenosphere, creating a trench on the surface and generating earthquakes with each jerk and jolt of its descent. Subduction zones usually lie near continental coastlines or arc-shaped island chains. The earthquakes that plague the Pacific coast of South America, for instance, originate in the Peru-Chile trench, where the South American plate pushes the Nazca plate into the mantle.

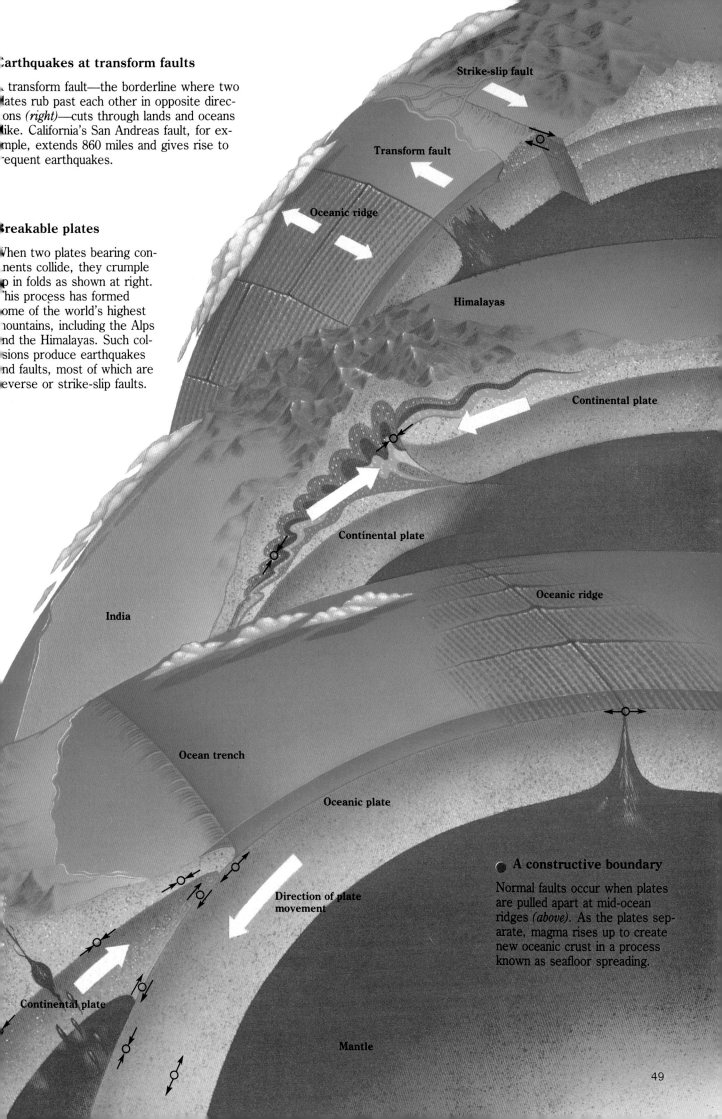

Earthquakes at transform faults

A transform fault—the borderline where two plates rub past each other in opposite directions *(right)*—cuts through lands and oceans alike. California's San Andreas fault, for example, extends 860 miles and gives rise to frequent earthquakes.

Breakable plates

When two plates bearing continents collide, they crumple up in folds as shown at right. This process has formed some of the world's highest mountains, including the Alps and the Himalayas. Such collisions produce earthquakes and faults, most of which are reverse or strike-slip faults.

Strike-slip fault

Transform fault

Oceanic ridge

Himalayas

Continental plate

Continental plate

Oceanic ridge

India

Ocean trench

Oceanic plate

Direction of plate movement

Continental plate

Mantle

A constructive boundary

Normal faults occur when plates are pulled apart at mid-ocean ridges *(above)*. As the plates separate, magma rises up to create new oceanic crust in a process known as seafloor spreading.

49

How Do Seismic Waves Travel?

When an earthquake jolts the rock along a fault, the shock is transmitted by vibrations called seismic waves; these travel outward in all directions from the quake's focus, or underground point of origin. Like ripples from a stone dropped in a pond, the waves spread concentrically. Some travel through the Earth's interior, while others move along its surface.

Using recording instruments known as seismographs, geologists have identified three basic types of seismic waves. The first vibrations to reach a seismograph are compressional waves, called primary, or P, waves. Like sound waves traveling through air, P waves move through rock by elastically compressing and expanding the rock itself. The next waves to arrive are the secondary, or S, waves, also known as shear waves. S waves move through rock with an up-and-down motion. When P and S waves reach the surface, some of them are transformed into a third type of seismic wave: surface waves.

Although P waves pass readily through solids and fluids, S waves can move only through solids. In general, the harder and denser the rock, the faster both types of waves travel through it. P waves take about 19 minutes to reach the opposite side of the Earth. S waves are stopped at the boundary of Earth's liquid outer core, where their energy is probably converted to heat. Surface waves are the slowest and most damaging of all; they may circle the globe several times before abating.

Have quake, will travel

Seismic waves radiate in three dimensions from the focus of an earthquake. Waves that reach the surface spread out in concentric circles from the epicenter—the spot on the ground that lies directly above the focus.

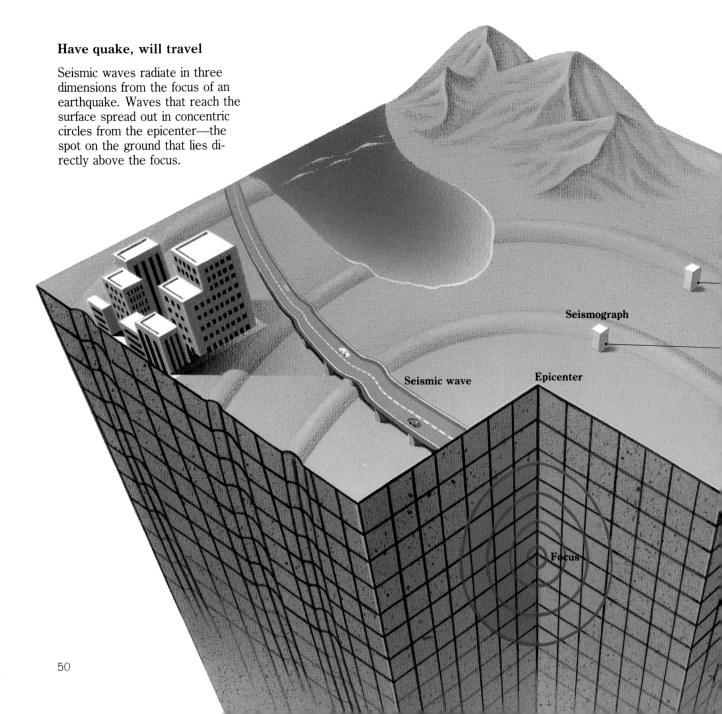

Seismograph

Seismic wave

Epicenter

Focus

Four waves that shake the world

Because they pass through the body of the planet, P and S waves are often referred to as body waves. P waves are the fastest; they move 4 miles per second by alternately compressing and stretching the material they travel through. S waves are only half that fast; their motion through the ground resembles the cracking of a whip. Surface waves, of which there are two varieties, affect the Earth's exterior only. Love waves snap back and forth horizontally like seismic sidewinders. Rayleigh waves churn up and down like ocean breakers.

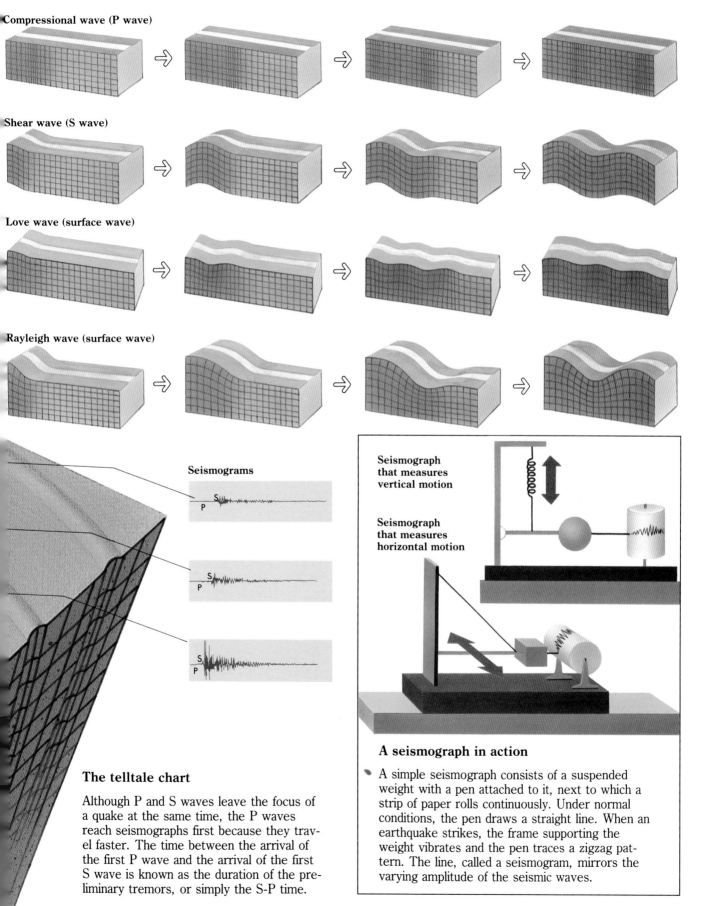

Compressional wave (P wave)

Shear wave (S wave)

Love wave (surface wave)

Rayleigh wave (surface wave)

Seismograms

Seismograph that measures vertical motion

Seismograph that measures horizontal motion

The telltale chart

Although P and S waves leave the focus of a quake at the same time, the P waves reach seismographs first because they travel faster. The time between the arrival of the first P wave and the arrival of the first S wave is known as the duration of the preliminary tremors, or simply the S-P time.

A seismograph in action

● A simple seismograph consists of a suspended weight with a pen attached to it, next to which a strip of paper rolls continuously. Under normal conditions, the pen draws a straight line. When an earthquake strikes, the frame supporting the weight vibrates and the pen traces a zigzag pattern. The line, called a seismogram, mirrors the varying amplitude of the seismic waves.

How Is the Focus Pinpointed?

For scientists trying to find the location of an earthquake's focus, the time delay between the arrival of P waves and S waves is a key piece of evidence. This interval, known as the S-P time, is computed by seismographs inside recording stations. The S-P time can be as short as a few seconds or as long as several minutes, but it always reveals the distance from the recording station to the epicenter.

Knowing the distance to the epicenter, however, is a far cry from knowing its origin. To zero in on this site, seismologists compute the epicenter's distance from at least three recording stations. A circle is then drawn around each station, with the circle's radius equaling the station's distance from the epicenter. The epicenter lies in the area where the circles overlap.

Although supercomputers help seismologists pinpoint the epicenter and calculate the exact depth of the focus, the positions can also be approximated by hand. The formula for doing so is explained on the opposite page.

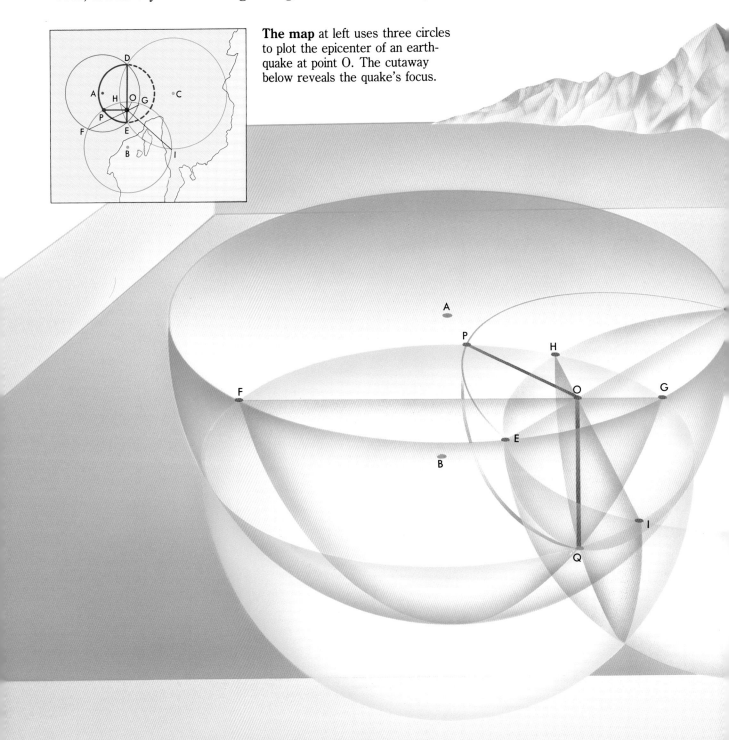

The map at left uses three circles to plot the epicenter of an earthquake at point O. The cutaway below reveals the quake's focus.

A focus-finding formula

The Omori formula is a reliable way to find an earthquake's focus. The formula is R = Kt, where R is the distance from the seismograph to the epicenter, K is a constant of 4.2 miles per second, and t is the S-P time.

First, the S-P time recorded at point A *(below, left)* is plugged into the equation. Second, this distance is reduced to map scale and used as the radius to draw a circle centered on point A. Third, similar circles are drawn around points B and C. Fourth, lines called common chords are drawn, linking the intersections of the circles; the lines intersect at point O—the epicenter.

To find the focus, a semicircle is drawn with a diameter equal to a common chord—for example, DE. A perpendicular line is then drawn from point O to the semicircle, intersecting it at point P. The distance of this segment, OP, reveals the depth of the focus.

Intervals between P and S waves

As shown below, the time delay between the arrival of P waves and the arrival of S waves increases with distance from the focus. The S-P time is thus constantly proportional to the distance from the focus.

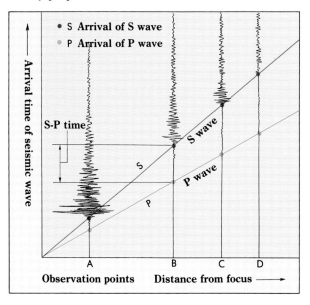

An isochronal bull's-eye

The moment at which a seismic wave reaches a given point on the Earth's surface is known as the time of occurrence. When points with the same time of occurrence are connected by lines called isochrones *(maps below)*, a series of concentric circles appear. At the center of these circles is the epicenter. The greater the distance between isochrones, the deeper the focus.

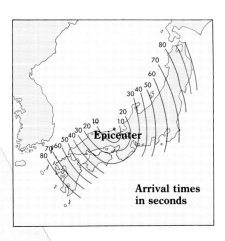

Arrival times in seconds

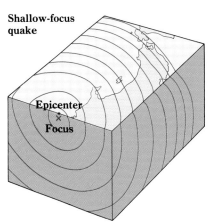

Shallow-focus quake

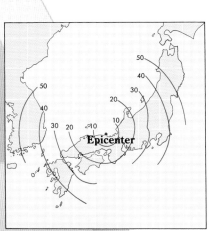

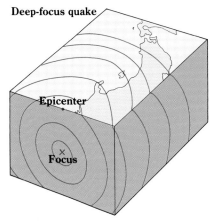

Deep-focus quake

What Happens during an Earthquake?

The most immediate effect of an earthquake is the shaking of the ground by seismic waves. In a minor tremor, the agitation lasts but a few seconds and may be barely detectable; in a severe one, the ground can seethe for several minutes. During the Kwanto earthquake of 1923, which all but destroyed the Japanese cities of Tokyo and Yokohama, the ground shuddered for a period of almost five minutes.

Most of the damage inflicted by a quake stems from these surface convulsions. But a temblor has a wide range of side effects as well, a sampling of which are shown below.

Cape Nojima *(above)*, on the tip of Japan's Chiba Peninsula, formed during the Kwanto earthquake of 1923, which fused the island of Nojima to the mainland.

Earthshaking events

Tsunami

Fissure

Aftershocks

Faulting. A shallow-focus earthquake often rips a fissure in the Earth *(above)*, throwing roads and other surface features out of kilter.

Flooding. A tremor that takes place under water can trigger a tsunami—an enormous sea wave that races across the ocean at speeds of up to 600 miles per hour. By the time it crashes inland, wreaking extensive destruction, the tsunami may tower 50 feet or more in height.

Echoing. A major quake is often followed by many smaller tremors known as aftershocks *(above)*. Thought to release any energy still in the rocks, aftershocks occur in parts of the fault where the original quake took place.

A face-lifting fault

Earthquakes can drastically alter the topography of a region. The earthquake of September 1923, the worst in Japan's history, touched off land upheavals, subsidence, and lateral shears throughout the Kwanto region. The floor of Tokyo Bay rose 10 feet higher, while the Izu Peninsula was shoved 13 feet to the west.

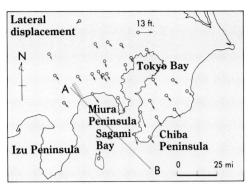

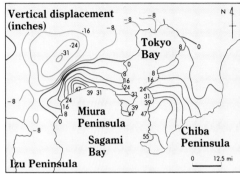

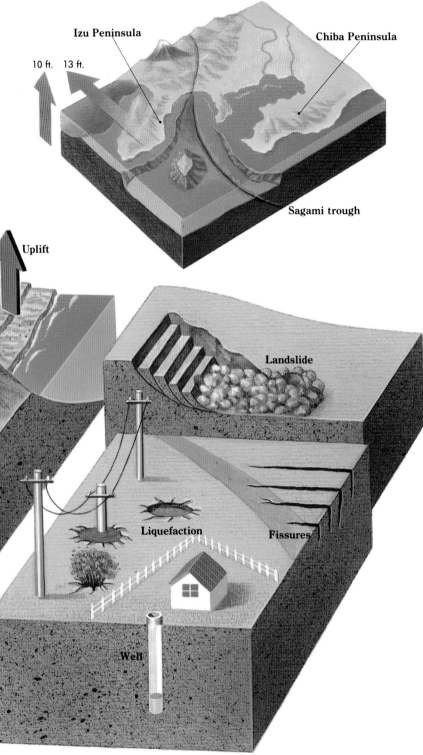

The maps above show the lateral and vertical displacement caused by the Kwanto earthquake of 1923. Line AB in the upper map represents the Sagami trough, which connects to a fault on land and is believed to have sparked the cataclysm. The lower map shows that the tips of the Miura and Chiba peninsulas were thrust more than 4 feet upward by the quake, while the Tanzawa mountain sank 2½ feet lower into the ground.

The fissure shown above opened in a California highway during the Loma Prieta earthquake of 1989. Fissures and landslides usually occur in soil containing large amounts of clay, sand, or silt, which have weak bonding properties.

luctuating. During an earthquake, water levels and flow rates n wells may rise or fall; the temerature of the water may change s well. These variations may one ay help predict earthquakes.

Fluidizing. Earthquake vibrations can liquefy sandy soils instantly, giving them the consistency of quicksand. The liquefaction causes sinking and slippage of the land.

Can Earthquakes Be Predicted?

By studying areas of the world with a high risk of earthquakes, scientists have identified a variety of phenomena that precede a major shock. Increasing numbers of small earthquakes and crustal movements are two such omens, as are the swelling or tilting of the ground and fluctuations in the magnetic properties of rocks. Changes in tide and ground-water levels may also portend a tremor. Even variations in animal behavior have sometimes been reported before an earthquake.

Using instruments like the ones shown below, researchers can measure a number of these warning signs. In a few instances, the resulting data have been used to foretell an earthquake. Unfortunately, the indicators can also be misleading: Not only do they differ from one tremor to the next, but some quakes also appear to strike out of the blue. A reliable method of determining when and where a quake will hit—and how strong it will be—has yet to be developed.

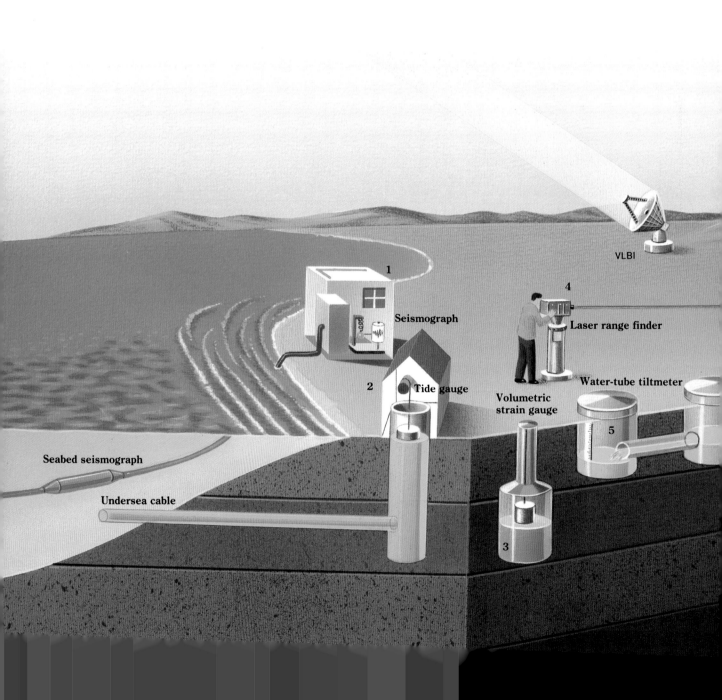

VLBI

1 Seismograph

4 Laser range finder

2 Tide gauge

Volumetric strain gauge

Water-tube tiltmeter

5

Seabed seismograph

Undersea cable

3

The tools of prediction

1. Seismographs provide instant detection of tremors. On the seabed, they are housed in pressure-resistant cases and linked to undersea cables.

2. A tide gauge relies on a float. A drop in tide level indicates an upheaval in the Earth's crust; a tide-level rise indicates subsidence.

3. In a volumetric strain gauge, buried in bedrock, the changing level of fluid reflects the contraction and expansion of the Earth's crust.

4. A laser range finder measures the distance between two points on opposite sides of a fault. If the fault moves, the distance changes.

5. A tiltmeter comprises two water-filled vessels joined by a pipe. Water-level changes signal a tilt in the crust.

6. A creep meter measures the slow, steady fault movement known as creep. A highly sensitive wire is stretched between two posts and across a fault. From one end of the wire hangs a free weight, which rises or falls as the fault moves.

7. A Geiger counter measures the radon gas dissolved in ground water, which increases before an earthquake.

8. In an extensometer, a quartz tube anchored at one end moves freely against a post at the other. When a quake causes the bedrock to expand or contract, the distance between the posts changes and is recorded by the movement of the tube's free end.

9. Very long-baseline interferometers (VLBIs) receive radio waves from quasars in space. Changes in the arrival times of the waves at different stations reveal crustal movements.

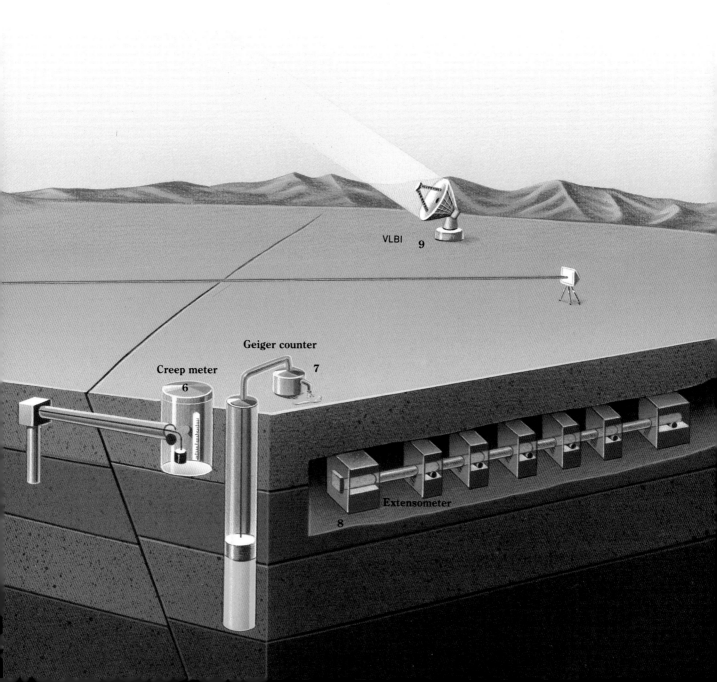

VLBI 9

Creep meter 6

Geiger counter 7

Extensometer 8

What Is a Tsunami?

When an underwater earthquake jolts the ocean floor, the sudden dislocation of the seabed and the resulting displacement of water can produce an immense, destructive wave known as a tsunami, which is Japanese for "harbor wave." Tsunamis race along at speeds of hundreds of miles an hour across the open ocean, where their crests may be 100 miles apart and their height only a few feet. As a tsunami enters shallower depths closer to land, however, it slows down and its wave height increases; finally, the towering wall of water slams into the coast. In narrow bays or inlets, which funnel and concentrate the energy of the waves, tsunamis have been known to surge as high as 90 feet before breaking.

The trail of a tsunami

1. When the ocean floor shifts along a fault, it displaces a huge amount of seawater. This generates the wave motion that becomes a tsunami.
2. A newly formed tsunami has an extremely long wavelength. Its height is so small that the wave can pass unnoticed beneath ships at sea.
3. As the tsunami nears land, the increasingly shallow seabed begins to act like a brake on the lower part of the wave.
4. Just offshore, the bottom of the wave slows down, but the crest bunches higher and higher until it rushes onto dry land. The faster the depth decreases, the greater the force of the tsunami.

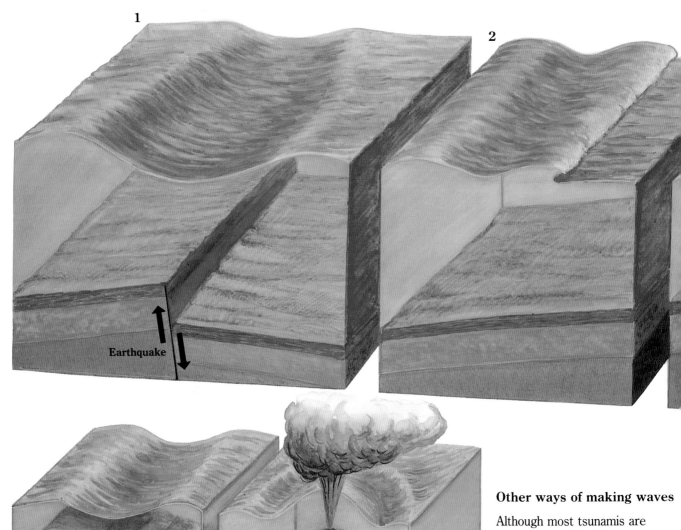

Other ways of making waves

Although most tsunamis are caused by earthquakes, some are created by landslides on the seabed *(far left)*. A tsunami may also result from the eruption of a submarine volcano *(left)*.

Landslide

Volcano

A deadly trek

The earthquake that struck the coast of Chile on May 23, 1960, triggered a tsunami that raced across the Pacific Ocean at 480 miles an hour (map, right). Some 14 hours later, the sea wave struck Hawaii; there it devastated Hilo harbor (below), causing an estimated $23 million in damage and killing 61 people.

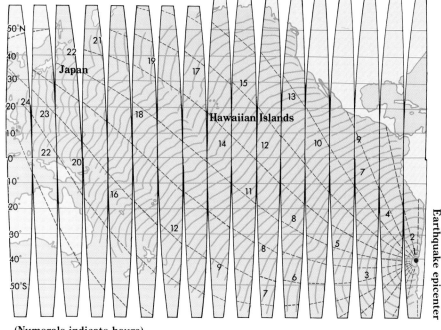

(Numerals indicate hours)

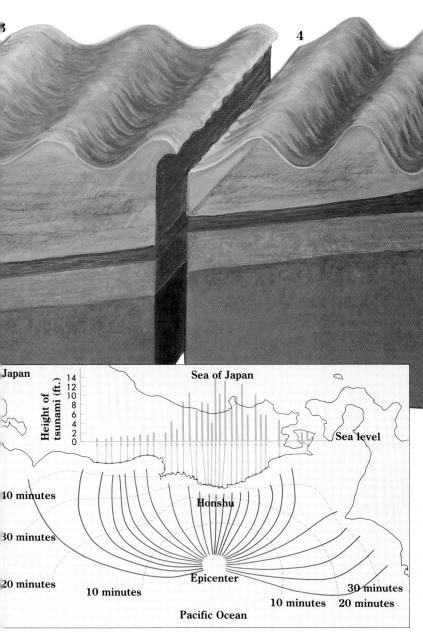

Bashing Japan

Of all the tsunamis that have pummeled the eastern coast of Honshu, the most devastating occurred in 1933. Spawned by an earthquake near the Japan trench on March 2, the tsunami propagated, or traveled outward, as shown by the dotted blue lines at left. It reached a height of 45 feet and killed 3,064 people.

59

What Is Ground Liquefaction?

The violent shaking that occurs during an earthquake can liquefy layers of soil near the surface. This liquefaction, as the process is called, usually affects filled land and other areas that sit atop wet, sandy soils. The moist foundation is normally stable enough to support overlying materials or structures. Seismic vibrations, however, agitate the particles in the soil, reducing it to a mush that resembles quicksand. If the pressure is high enough, the liquefied soil may spurt out of cracks in the ground.

Liquefaction causes an array of collateral damage, including subsidence, flowage, and landslides. During the earthquake that hit Niigata, Japan, in 1964, apartment buildings sank 6 feet into the ground as the surface beneath them liquefied and gave way. Water mains and gas lines buried in the subsoil were ruptured as well. The Loma Prieta earthquake, which rocked the San Francisco region in 1989, touched off severe liquefaction—and major damage—in areas of filled land.

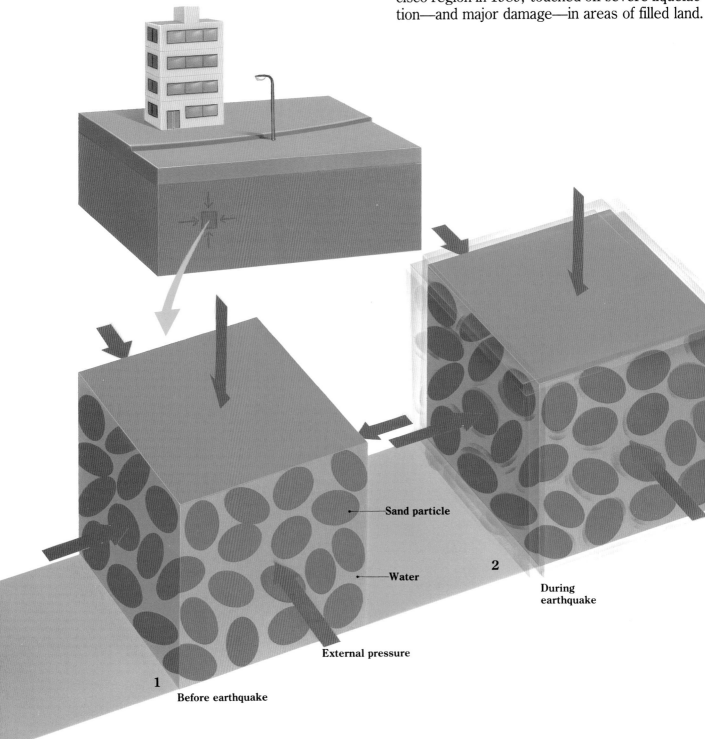

Sand particle

Water

External pressure

2
During
earthquake

1
Before earthquake

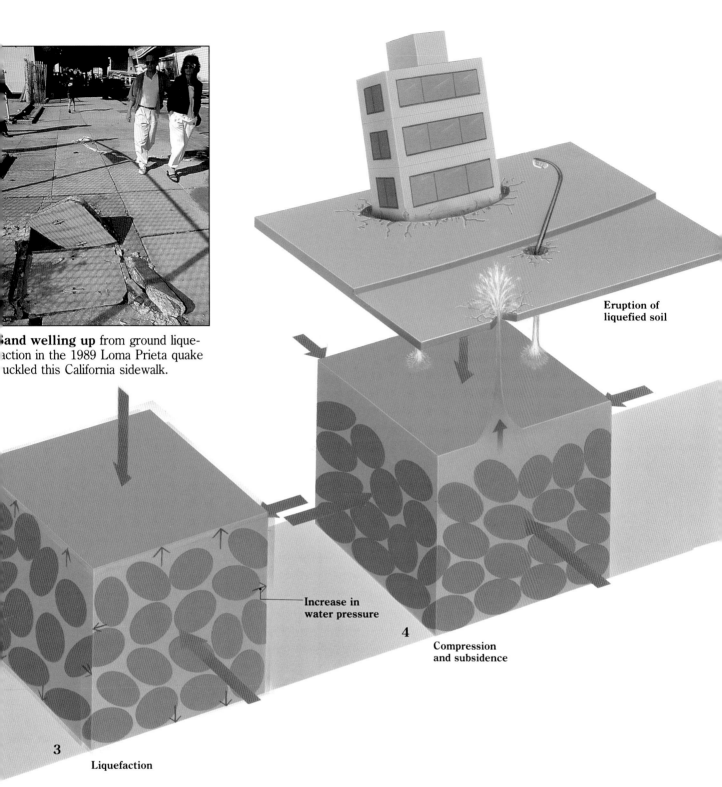

Sand welling up from ground liquefaction in the 1989 Loma Prieta quake
buckled this California sidewalk.

**Eruption of
liquefied soil**

**Increase in
water pressure**

4

**Compression
and subsidence**

3

Liquefaction

Settling down

1. Ordinarily, water fills the spaces between
particles of sandy soil. The pressure that the
particles and the water exert on one another
supports the soil against external pressure.
2. During a quake, prolonged vibrations
make the soil assume the properties of a
dense liquid; this disturbs the grain-to-grain
support between sand particles.
3. With the sand particles suspended in the
water, the soil loses its strength. Increased
pressure from the earthquake may cause the
water pressure to rise abruptly.
4. To relieve the pressure, the water rises
toward the surface, causing the soil to liquefy into a quicksandlike substance. The subsoil is compacted, and subsidence occurs.

The Loma Prieta quake

Although the epicenter of
California's 1989 Loma Prieta
earthquake lay some 60 miles
south of San Francisco, the
shock damaged the city and
its surroundings by means of
liquefaction. In unstable areas
of filled land on the shores of
San Francisco Bay, liquefaction caused many apartment
buildings to sink into the
ground or topple over. Liquefaction also prompted the
collapse of a 1.6-mile stretch
of elevated freeway in the
nearby city of Oakland.

San Francisco

Pacific
Ocean

Airport

Hayward fault

San Andreas fault

Epicenter ⊗

Santa Cruz

Areas of ground
liquefaction

4

Volcanoes: Earth's Power Unleashed

Nothing evokes the boundless energies of Earth more awesomely than an erupting volcano. Creators and destroyers, volcanoes can transform land, sea, and sky. During a six-day period in 1943, a ground vent spewing cinders in a field in Paricutín, Mexico, grew into a 500-foot volcanic cone; over the next nine years, the new volcano added 1,000 feet to its height and buried the nearby town of San Juan under ash. In 1883 the eruption of Krakatoa in Indonesia swallowed an island and blasted so much volcanic dust into the atmosphere that regions in faraway Europe suffered a 10 percent decrease in sunlight for three years.

But not all volcanoes are violent. Hawaii's Kilauea, for example, calmly oozes abundant lava, depositing volcanic rock on the island's southern coast and extending Hawaii's reach into the sea. And in Iceland, molten rock flows quietly from fissures, or cracks in the ground, to create lava plains.

Such volcanic land building has been going on since Earth's infancy; in fact, volcanoes have forged more than 80 percent of the world's continents and seabeds. Even the oceans and the air evolved from volcanic gases disgorged over millions of years.

This chapter explores why volcanoes arise, how they erupt, and what humans are doing to minimize their destructive potential. It also examines some of the natural wonders that are side effects of volcanism.

A fiery curtain of lava rises from a fissure on Mount Mihara, a volcano on Japan's Oshima Island. In the early 1990s, the volcano was the site of violent summit outbursts and Hawaiian-style flank eruptions *(page 66)*.

How Is Lava Formed?

The lava spewed out by a volcano *(right)* originates deep inside the Earth. As explained in Chapter 2, Earth's continental and oceanic plates ride on the upper mantle, a layer of somewhat plastic rock surrounding Earth's superheated core. As the plates collide and separate, narrow but deep vertical openings called fissures often develop in the crust. The interaction of the plates also generates a supply of underground magma, or molten rock *(below)*. The magma follows the fissures to the surface, where volcanoes expel it as hot lava.

▲ **Hawaii's Mount Kilauea** belches cinders and glowing lava from a magma reservoir.

Volcano

Continental plate

Magma reservoir

Mantle

Oceanic plate

● **Inside a lava factory**

Magma forms when the rock of an oceanic plate, forced deep inside the Earth by an overriding continental plate, comes in contact with the mantle and melts. This creates hot, buoyant magma that rises through the mantle in tadpole-shaped bubbles. Upon reaching the crust, the magma collects in reservoirs that lie just below the surface.

Rising magma

Lava's key ingredient

Whether lava is gooey like tar or fluid like syrup depends on how much silica—a crystalline rock—it contains. Kilauea's lava (right) has only 51 percent silica, making it liquid and quick.

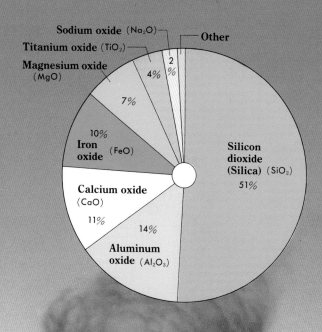

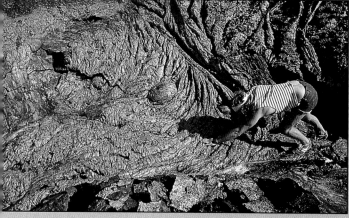

A geologist studies pahoehoe lava—a runny, low-silica mixture with a surface that cools rapidly, creating a ropy flow.

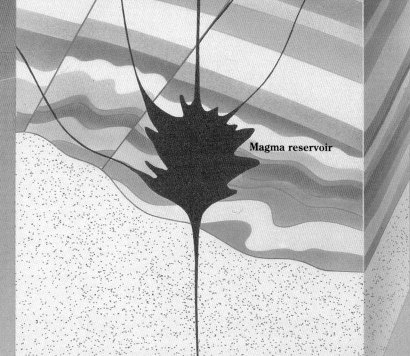

Ocean trench

Magma conduit

Magma reservoir

A recipe for disaster

A volcano erupts when the pressure of the subsurface magma exceeds the pressure of the overlying rock. Churning like boiling soup in its shallow reservoir, the magma is buoyed by water vapor and other hot gases; these help the magma migrate through cracks and vents toward the surface.

Why Do Volcanoes Differ?

The Earth's 516 active volcanoes come in all shapes and sizes, and each has its own style of erupting. Hawaii's Mount Kilauea, for example, quietly exudes low-lying floods of lava, while Italy's Vesuvius emits sky-splitting fireworks.

These varied eruptions, illustrated below, result from differences in the magma that each volcano contains. A magma that is low in gas and silica yields a gentle flow of thin, quickly spreading lava. A magma that is rich in gas and silica, by contrast, gives rise to violent explosions: The tarlike magma may plug up the volcanic vent, blocking any upward movement from below until pressure in the vapor-charged lava blows away the overlying rock.

The size and shape of a volcano depend on its eruptive history. As shown at right, free-flowing vents and fissures build lava plateaus or sloping shield volcanoes; cataclysmic eruptions create craterlike calderas.

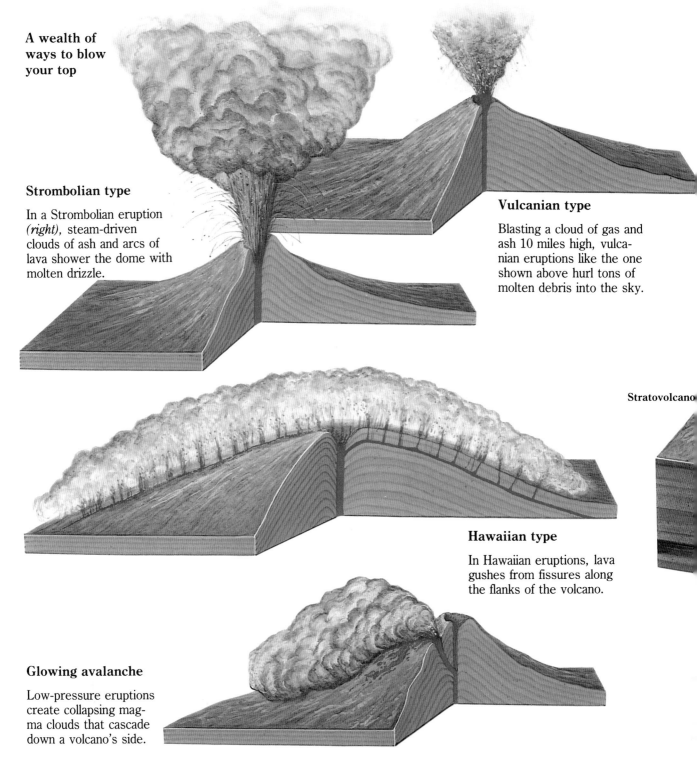

A wealth of ways to blow your top

Strombolian type

In a Strombolian eruption *(right),* steam-driven clouds of ash and arcs of lava shower the dome with molten drizzle.

Vulcanian type

Blasting a cloud of gas and ash 10 miles high, vulcanian eruptions like the one shown above hurl tons of molten debris into the sky.

Stratovolcano

Hawaiian type

In Hawaiian eruptions, lava gushes from fissures along the flanks of the volcano.

Glowing avalanche

Low-pressure eruptions create collapsing magma clouds that cascade down a volcano's side.

The many faces of volcanoes

Volcanoes assume varied shapes (below) according to the composition of their magmas and their past eruptions.

Cinder cone

The simplest volcano—the cinder cone—grows up around an explosive central vent that expels magma cinders. As the cinders settle around the vent, they form a sloping dome with a bowl-shaped crater. Cinder cones are small, rarely exceeding 1,000 feet.

Maar volcano

A ground-hugging eruption of magmatic gases sometimes creates a maar—a shallow crater 200 to 6,500 feet wide.

Lava plateau

Runny lava oozing from transverse fissures in the crust collects in vast pools; over the eons, these lava lakes solidify into mile-thick plateaus of volcanic rock. Such plateaus compose much of India's Deccan Peninsula.

Shield volcano

A shield volcano, built layer by layer from many watery, low-silica lava flows, is among the world's largest. The lava accumulates in dense layers, forming a low-angled mountain topped by a quietly erupting magma vent. A shield volcano can be 3 to 4 miles across and 2,000 feet high.

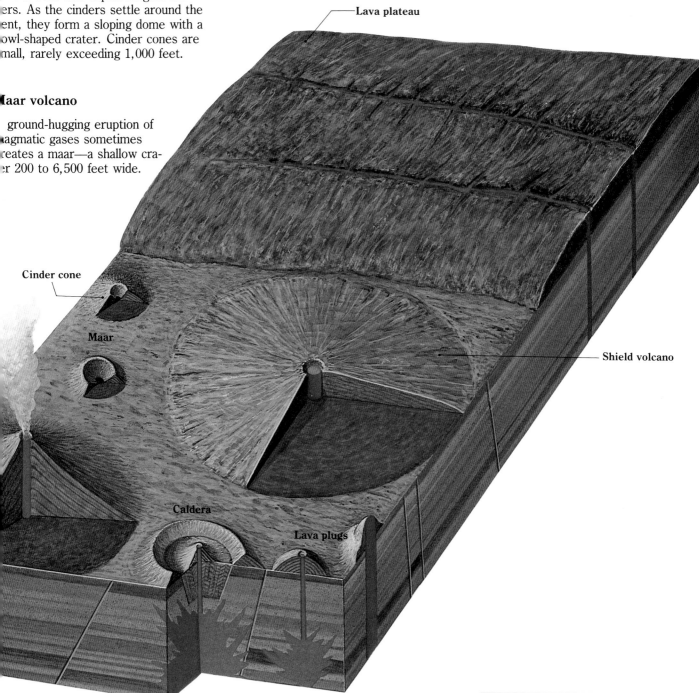

Lava plateau

Cinder cone

Maar

Shield volcano

Caldera

Lava plugs

Stratovolcano

A stratovolcano consists of alternating strata, or layers, of ash and lava. Washington's Mount St. Helens and Japan's Mount Fuji typify these steep cones, which may have one or more magma vents on their summits or flanks.

Lava plug

A pillar of rigid, semi-cooled lava that squeezes from a magma vent is called a lava plug. Japan's Showa New Mountain (right) formed in 1945 from such a column.

What Is a Caldera?

Hawaii's Kilauea is one of the world's most active volcanoes, but its eruptions are so tame that sightseers have stood on the volcano's rim to watch them occur. Kilauea is a lofty mountain topped by a caldera—a large, bowl-shaped volcanic crater. In 1924 the volcano vented its entire magma reservoir in a series of 41 flaming eruptions. The cone then sank into the vacant magma chamber, creating a crater. Across the floor of this crater there soon sprouted tiny cones and fissures; from these trickle the lazy lava flows that are tourist attractions.

Some calderas form suddenly rather than gradually: They take shape when a volcano blows its top and empties its magma reservoir in one monstrous spasm. Afterward, as the magma reservoir fills with debris and solidifies, a volcano of this type may cease to erupt altogether.

Oregon's Crater Lake *(above),* one of the largest calderas, is 6 miles wide. Its walls are 2,000 feet high.

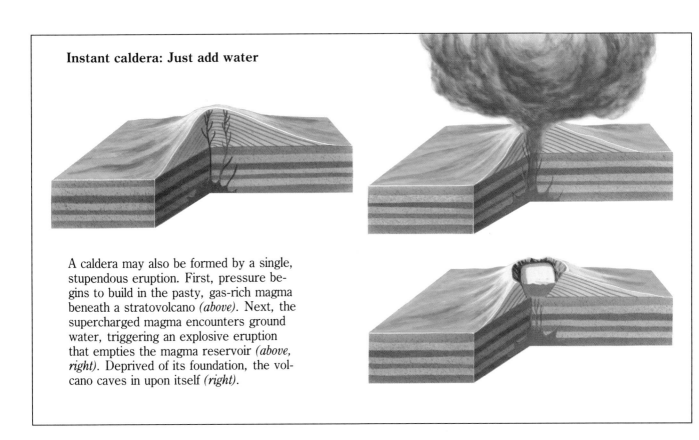

Instant caldera: Just add water

A caldera may also be formed by a single, stupendous eruption. First, pressure begins to build in the pasty, gas-rich magma beneath a stratovolcano *(above).* Next, the supercharged magma encounters ground water, triggering an explosive eruption that empties the magma reservoir *(above, right).* Deprived of its foundation, the volcano caves in upon itself *(right).*

Creating a caldera

As shown in this sequence, most calderas result when a volcano collapses into a magma reservoir that has been drained by long eruptions.

1 **A caldera** starts forming as repeated eruptions begin to deplete the volcano's magma supply. The gas pressure in the magma chamber drops.

2 **As the magma** level declines, ash eruptions continue. This further lowers the gas pressure in the magma chamber.

3 **Once the gas** pressure in the magma chamber drops below a certain point, the volcano can no longer support the cone. Like a house crumbling into its basement, the volcano slumps into the hollow reservoir below, creating a crater-shaped cavity.

4 **If magma** percolates into fractures beneath the collapsed volcano, small volcanoes may form on the caldera floor. Water may collect into a lake.

How Did Mount St. Helens Erupt?

At 8:32 on the morning of May 18, 1980, Mount St. Helens in Washington erupted with the fury of 500 atomic bombs. A magma bulge on the volcano's north side popped like a bubble, releasing explosive gases and water. White-hot steam then blasted from the volcano's side, lopping 1,313 feet off the summit and flattening every tree within 15 miles. As 3 billion cubic yards of pulverized rock and ash hurtled down the mountain, the debris mixed with snow and ice to blanket the countryside in a runny ooze.

Snapped like twigs, dead trees surrounding Mount St. Helens testify to the force of the volcano's lateral eruption. Winds of 500° F. engulfed 232 square miles of forest, scorching bark and smothering the land with ash.

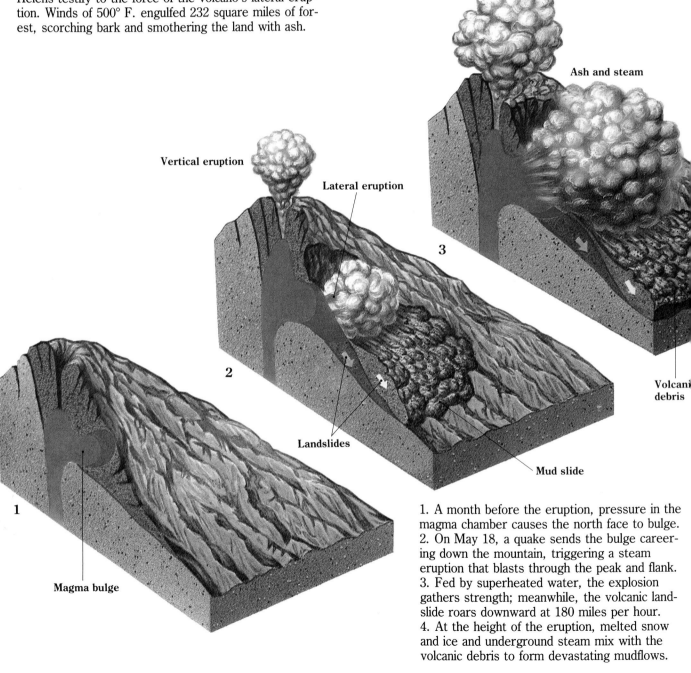

Ash and steam

Vertical eruption

Lateral eruption

3

Volcanic debris

Landslides

2

Mud slide

Magma bulge

1

1. A month before the eruption, pressure in the magma chamber causes the north face to bulge.
2. On May 18, a quake sends the bulge careering down the mountain, triggering a steam eruption that blasts through the peak and flank.
3. Fed by superheated water, the explosion gathers strength; meanwhile, the volcanic landslide roars downward at 180 miles per hour.
4. At the height of the eruption, melted snow and ice and underground steam mix with the volcanic debris to form devastating mudflows.

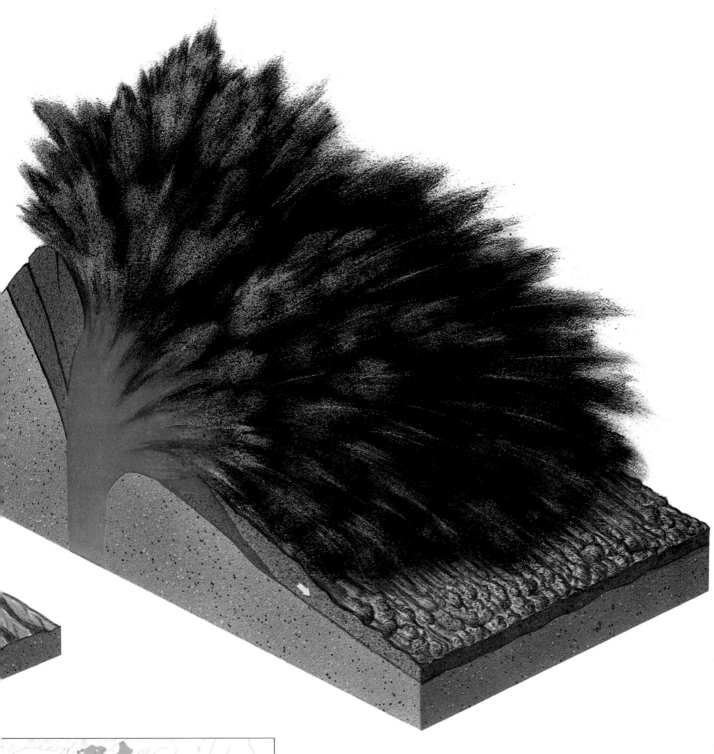

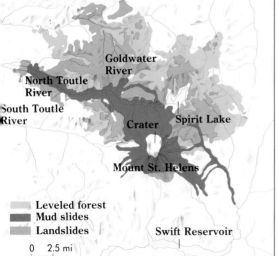

An avalanche of rock, ash, and ice roared down
valleys, felling enough timber for 250,000 homes.

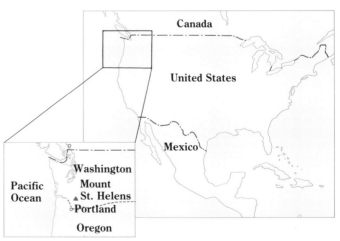

Mount St. Helens provided deadly evidence that many
volcanoes in the Cascade Range are only temporarily quiet.

71

What Was Krakatoa's Eruption Like?

August 27, 1883: It had been a morning of terrifying eruptions, but now Krakatoa—a volcanic island in Indonesia—fell strangely silent. Just as people thought the worst had passed, a deafening roar split the air and 5 cubic miles of glowing rock and cinders jetted skyward. With a colossal shudder, two of Krakatoa's 1,000-foot peaks sank beneath the seas, forming a 900-foot-deep caldera. The displaced seawater created 130-foot waves that wiped out 295 towns and killed 36,000 people. Airborne ash plunged areas 50 miles away into two days of inky dark, while enormous cinder-rafts settled on the seas. Three years later, a veil of volcanic debris still hung in the air.

Steam and ash rise from Anak Krakatoa ("child of Krakatoa"), a volcanic island that began forming in 1927 on the floor of the Krakatoa caldera.

Crack goes Krakatoa

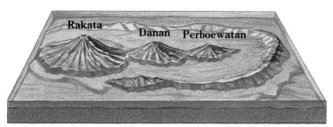

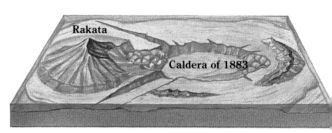

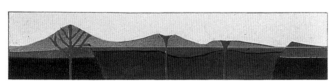

Before it erupted in 1883, the island of Krakatoa comprised three volcanic peaks—Rakata, Danan, and Perboewatan—surrounded by the rim of an ancient caldera *(above, left)*. After the cataclysm *(above, right)*, only Rakata remained; Danan and Perboewatan had disappeared below the ocean, leaving behind a fresh caldera.

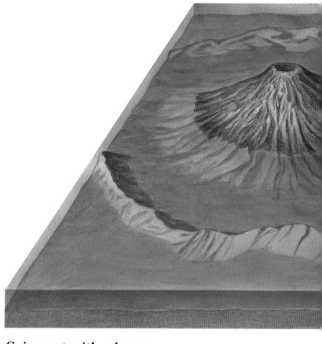

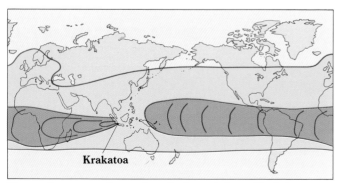

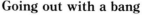

Borne by easterly trade winds, ash from Krakatoa circled the globe in two weeks *(purple)*. It then spread out for a second pass *(pink)* before dissipating.

Going out with a bang

Throughout the day on August 26, 1883, a series of explosive eruptions rocked the tiny volcanic island of Krakatoa. By 2:00 p.m., the twin peaks of Danan and Perboewatan had belched a monstrous black cloud that rained ash and hot pumice on the surrounding region. Krakatoa's

Volcanic debris

feverish spasms intensified through the night and into the morning. Finally, at 10:02 a.m. on August 27, a titanic steam explosion convulsed Krakatoa, blowing an ash cloud 50 miles high and swallowing two-thirds of the Indonesian island.

Krakatoa created killer tsunamis *(pages 58-59),* which reached nearby islands within 25 minutes of the volcano's eruption.

How Was Pompeii Buried?

The oldest written account of a volcanic eruption describes the destruction of Pompeii and Herculaneum, towns on Italy's Bay of Naples, by Mount Vesuvius in AD 79. Although Pompeii was a well-known city in Roman times, the town was lost to history for nearly 1,700 years, buried under layers of fine ash and pumice—a frothy volcanic rock—thrown out by Vesuvius. Not until 1748, when construction workers unearthed parts of the ancient city, was Pompeii rediscovered. Protected from the elements by its airless blanket of ash, Pompeii emerged strangely intact—much as it was on the morning Vesuvius erupted.

Pompeii, at the foot of Vesuvius, was 100 miles from Rome.

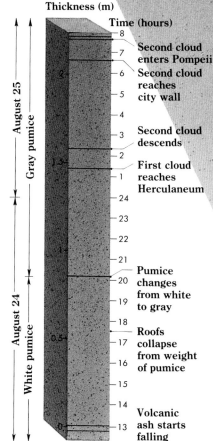

Vesuvius, August 24

Unearthed after nearly two millennia, the Roman city of Pompeii stands again in the shadow of its destroyer, Mount Vesuvius. Three-fifths of the once-grand city has been excavated.

Pots and cooking vessels, left as they were at the moment Vesuvius blew, still grace a kitchen in Pompeii.

Thickness (m)

Time (hours)

- 8
- 7 — Second cloud enters Pompeii
- 6 — Second cloud reaches city wall
- 5
- 4
- 3 — Second cloud descends
- 2
- 1 — First cloud reaches Herculaneum
- 24
- 23
- 22
- 21
- 20 — Pumice changes from white to gray
- 19
- 18
- 17 — Roofs collapse from weight of pumice
- 16
- 15
- 14
- 13 — Volcanic ash starts falling

August 25 / Gray pumice

August 24 / White pumice

A diagramed cross section of excavated earth *(left)* shows the types and thickness of volcanic debris laid down hour by hour during the eruption.

Sulfurous clouds, cindery ash, and hail-size pumice spread over regions with the misfortune to lie downwind of Vesuvius.

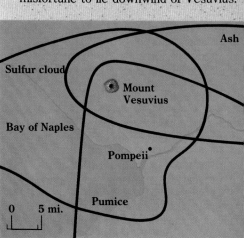

Ash

Sulfur cloud

Mount Vesuvius

Bay of Naples

Pompeii

Pumice

0   5 mi.

Vesuvius, August 25

Pompeii

Pompeii

2

1. The eruption of AD 79 began with a thunderous clap, as Vesuvius blasted a column of hot ash 12 miles into the air. As the debris began to settle, a blizzard of dusty ash, pumice, and choking vapors descended on Pompeii.

2. A day later Vesuvius erupted with renewed violence, disgorging a glowing avalanche of superheated ash and pumice that gradually buried the city beneath 20 feet of volcanic waste.

▶ **The bodies** of Pompeians killed by the eruption decomposed inside sheaths of hardened ash; centuries later, these hollows were filled with plaster to re-create the once-living forms.

Where Do Seamounts Form?

In the 1950s sonar mapping began to reveal that about 10,000 volcanoes rise from the ocean floor. Some of these seamounts, as submerged volcanoes are called, are extinct; others continue to erupt with spectacular force. Below a depth of 1,000 feet, however, the weight of the seawater prevents the release of gases that make for explosive eruptions.

Although a submarine volcano can grow to measure 30,000 feet from base to peak, it starts out as a tiny seafloor vent. Such a vent normally occurs near the boundary between tectonic plates. Less often, it is found in the middle of a plate, over a stationary magma plume known as a hot spot *(pages 44-45)*. As the plate creeps over the hot spot, a chain of volcanic islands gradually forms.

Steam and rock explode skyward from a submarine volcano, heralding the birth of a new island.

Three ways to build a volcano at sea

Where oceanic plates collide *(below, left)*, magma erupts to form island-arc volcanoes. When two plates separate, magma seeps upward, creating ocean-ridge volcanoes near the rift *(right)*. A hot-spot volcano *(center)* takes shape when a torchlike plume melts rock in the upper mantle, producing magma that erupts as lava.

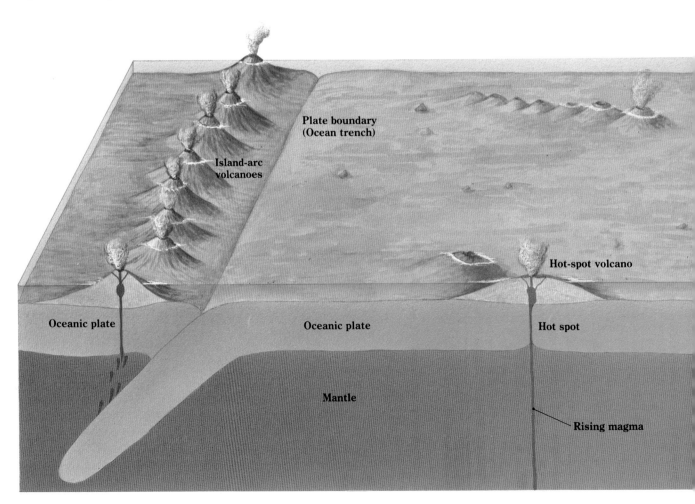

Plate boundary
(Ocean trench)

Island-arc
volcanoes

Hot-spot volcano

Oceanic plate

Oceanic plate

Hot spot

Mantle

Rising magma

How hot-spot volcanic islands are formed

1. Magma bubbling from a hot spot deposits pillow lava on the seafloor and heats the surrounding ocean.
2. The pillow lava piles up around the volcanic vent, forming a gently sloping cone.
3. The cone emerges from the sea. Gases in the magma expand, causing steam explosions. Glassy rubble and hardened cinders collect on the flanks of the slowly swelling volcanic cone.

4. The cone disgorges flows of fluid lava and becomes a full-blown shield volcano. Eventually, the volcano's summit may collapse to form a caldera.
5. Intermittent eruptions add to the volcano, enlarging the base of the new island. Waves and wind batter the volcanic rock into soil. After the volcano becomes extinct, millions of years of erosion will wear away its exposed surface, returning the island to the sea.

Now volcanically extinct, the islands of Maui *(bottom)* and Kahoolawe once straddled the hot spot where the island of Hawaii sits today. The islands were moved northwest by the Pacific plate.

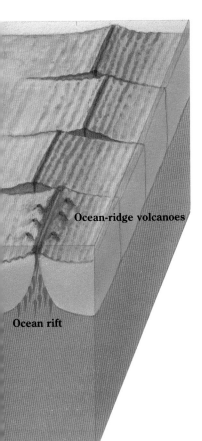

Ocean-ridge volcanoes

Ocean rift

1

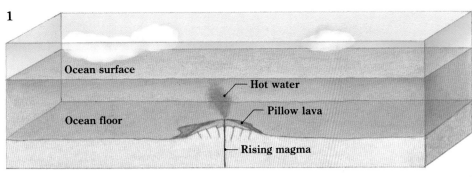

Ocean surface

Ocean floor

Hot water

Pillow lava

Rising magma

2

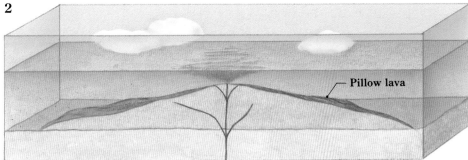

Pillow lava

3

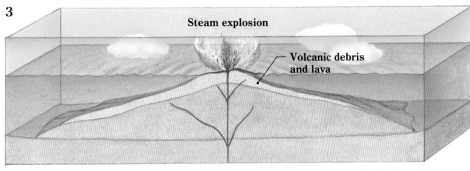

Steam explosion

Volcanic debris and lava

4

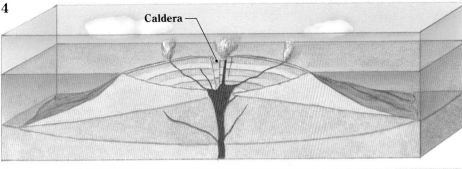

Caldera

5

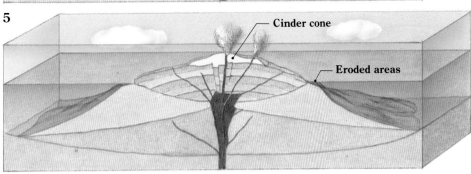

Cinder cone

Eroded areas

Can Eruptions Be Predicted?

The eruption of Mount St. Helens in May 1980 killed more than 60 people. Had scientists not warned local residents to leave the area beforehand, however, the death toll might have reached 30,000.

Many bits of evidence led to this life-saving prediction. In 1978, for example, a study of the volcano's history indicated an outburst was likely before the year 2000. Data from other volcanoes—frequent local earthquakes, a buildup of volcanic gases—yielded more clues suggesting Mount St. Helens would soon blow.

Today volcanologists are improving their methods of predicting eruptions. Using the instruments shown on these pages, they keep a constant watch on the vital signs of volcanoes. The results are encouraging: Between 1984 and 1986, geophysicists at the Hawaiian Volcano Observatory accurately forecast 47 eruptions on Mount Kilauea. Scientists at the University of Washington, meanwhile, have successfully predicted 90 percent of Mount St. Helens' outbursts since 1980.

Garbed in heat-resistant gear, a scientist collects lava for temperature and chemical analysis.

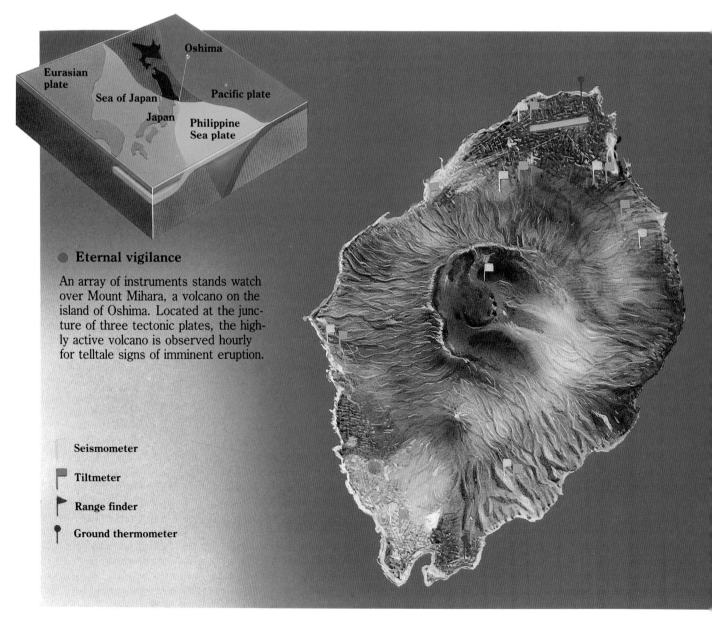

● **Eternal vigilance**

An array of instruments stands watch over Mount Mihara, a volcano on the island of Oshima. Located at the juncture of three tectonic plates, the highly active volcano is observed hourly for telltale signs of imminent eruption.

Seismometer

Tiltmeter

Range finder

Ground thermometer

An array of sensors

No two volcanoes are alike. To forecast when a given volcano will erupt, geologists must therefore study the volcano's structure and eruptive history. Then the scientists incorporate readings, taken by detectors such as those illustrated at right, of the volcano's earthquake activity, ground tilt, temperature, electric and gravitational properties, and gas output.

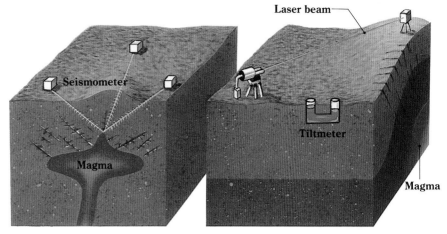

Seismometers

Seismometers on and around the volcano detect the location and intensity of earthquakes caused by the movement of magma.

Tiltmeters

Tiltmeters gauge changes in water levels or the travel time of a laser beam, which vary as magma flow raises or lowers ground elevation.

Close encounters

Standing behind a knee-high ridge of dried lava, a volcanologist collects samples of gases escaping from Kilauea, an active volcano on Hawaii. In the background is a gentle lava cascade.

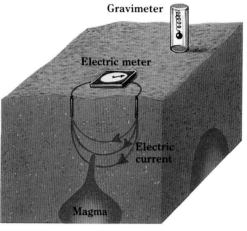

Electric and gravity meters

Magma conducts electric current, so scientists use electric meters to spot it rising. Gravimeters can also detect flowing magma.

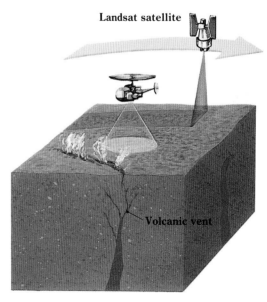

Taking temperatures and gauging gas

Landsat uses infrared sensors to detect temperature changes in volcanoes. Aircraft monitor gas discharge.

Geologists collect gas samples from a volcanic vent on Mount Baker, Washington. An increase in levels of sulfur dioxide and other gases signals an impending increase in volcanic activity.

Why Do Geysers Occur?

Geysers are hot springs that erupt at intervals ranging from minutes to days, spurting fountains of scalding water and steam as high as 200 feet in the air. Geysers are fueled by the same sort of forces that make volcanoes explode: First, heat transferred from magma to rocks turns underground water into pressurized steam; then, hissing upward through chinks where the crust is unusually thin, the steam periodically bursts through the surface.

Yellowstone National Park in the state of Wyoming boasts 72 geysers. Other geysers are clustered in Iceland and New Zealand, regions where the Earth's crust is no more than 2 to 3 miles thick.

Like a quirky clock, Old Faithful in Yellowstone Park spouts off every 65 minutes or so.

Yellowstone's steam generator

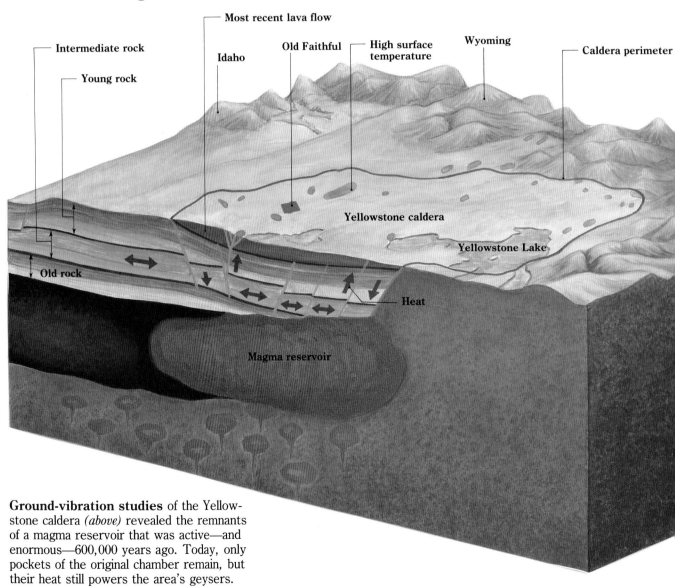

Ground-vibration studies of the Yellowstone caldera *(above)* revealed the remnants of a magma reservoir that was active—and enormous—600,000 years ago. Today, only pockets of the original chamber remain, but their heat still powers the area's geysers.

Geyser-making mechanisms

Though every geyser differs, scientists believe that all of them originate in one of the three ways illustrated at right.

Water in a shallow cavity

Beneath a cavity geyser is a hollow chamber in which ground water collects. Heat in the surrounding rocks slowly brings the water to a boil, causing it first to vaporize and then to erupt as steam.

Water in a vertical channel

A tube geyser is fed by a narrow channel containing water that is heated by hot rock along its path. As the water rises, some of it turns to steam, ejecting the water ahead of it.

Water in a thin layer

The moisture that fuels a water-layer geyser may pool in a thin stratum deep inside the Earth, where rocks heat it to more than 400° F. Only when the water nears the surface and pressure decreases will it boil and explode.

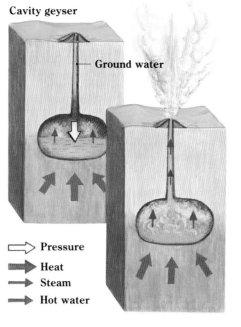

Cavity geyser

Ground water

Pressure

Heat

Steam

Hot water

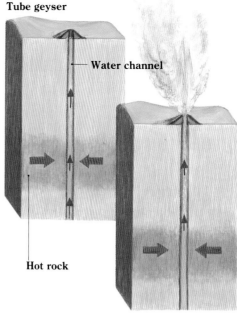

Tube geyser

Water channel

Hot rock

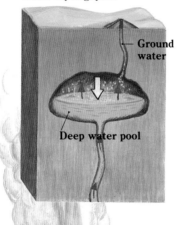
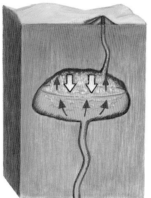
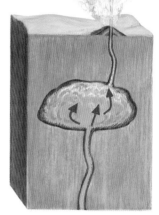

Water-layer geyser

Ground water

Deep water pool

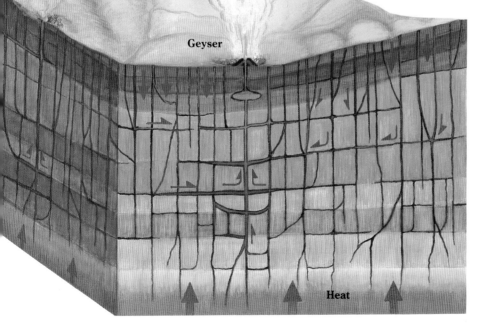

Hot spring

Geyser

Heat

The gestation of a geyser

Some 60 million years ago, three volcanic eruptions shattered the Yellowstone area, lacing the bedrock with seams and crevices. Today, cool ground water *(blue arrows)* trickles down through these cracks to a depth of a mile or more, where the remnant magma reservoir *(far left)* slowly heats it to several hundred degrees Fahrenheit. Made buoyant by this heat, the water then rises *(small red arrows)* through the broken rock. Near the surface, low pressures permit the superheated water to flash into steam and explode upward.

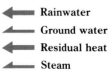

Rainwater

Ground water

Residual heat

Steam

How Do Hot Springs Form?

Hot springs—pools of steaming water often tinted red, yellow, green, or blue by minerals or algae—are formed in much the same way as geysers. Cool rainwater trickles down through honeycombed rock underground and is heated by magma. This hot, buoyant water then rises, dissolving minerals and other compounds and carrying them to the surface. There, bubbling gently from a crevice, the hot waters gather to form a spring. The dissolved minerals usually settle out of the water and build crusty deposits around the rim of the spring. Such geothermal springs, as they are called, vary in temperature, but many are hot enough to poach an egg.

Steam rises from a bubbling hot spring.

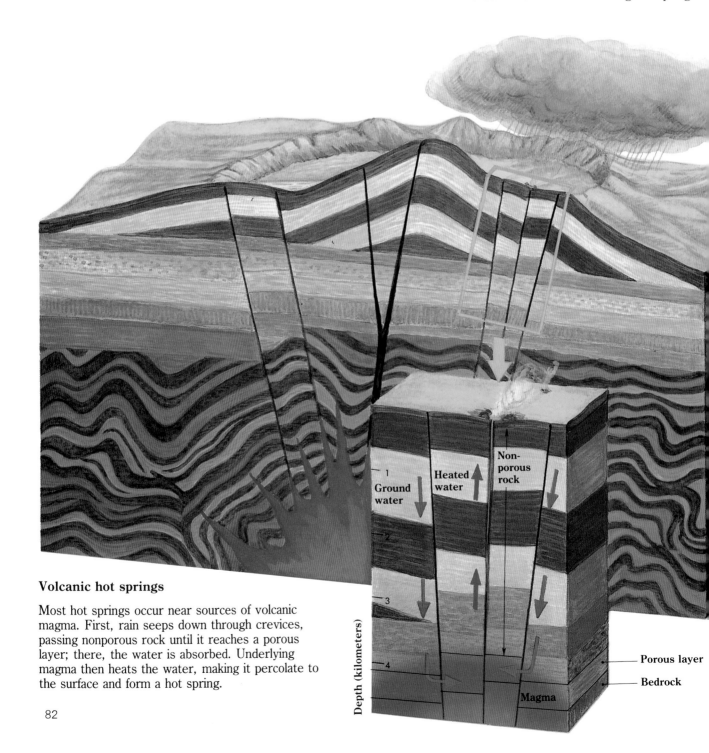

Volcanic hot springs

Most hot springs occur near sources of volcanic magma. First, rain seeps down through crevices, passing nonporous rock until it reaches a porous layer; there, the water is absorbed. Underlying magma then heats the water, making it percolate to the surface and form a hot spring.

Mapping hot zones

The worldwide distribution of geothermal springs *(right)* corresponds closely to that of volcanoes. Hot springs and volcanoes are both found near tectonic boundaries, where colliding or diverging plates stir up magma from deep in the Earth. This magma surges to the surface through volcanoes, while the heat it generates powers hot springs. Volcanoes and hot springs also are known to occur over mid-plate hot spots such as Hawaii.

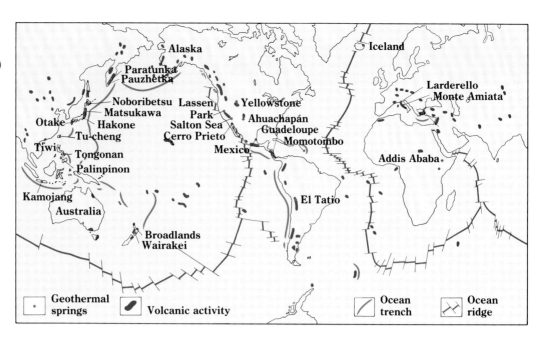

Alaska

Iceland

Paratunka
Pauzhetka

Noboribetsu Lassen Yellowstone
Matsukawa Park
Otake Hakone Salton Sea Ahuachapán
Tu-cheng Cerro Prieto Guadeloupe
Tiwi Mexico Momotombo
Tongonan
Palinpinon

Larderello
Monte Amiata

Addis Ababa

Kamojang
Australia

El Tatio

Broadlands
Wairakei

| · | **Geothermal springs** | | **Volcanic activity** | | | **Ocean trench** | | **Ocean ridge** |

Nonvolcanic hot springs

Occasionally, hot springs arise far from the site of any recent volcanic activity. The heat that fuels these nonvolcanic springs comes from such alternative sources as naturally radioactive elements, friction from sideslipping rock layers, and residual heat from ancient magma reservoirs.

Rain

Ground
water

Non-
porous
rock

Hot springs

Heated water

Ground water

Porous layer

Residual heat

5
Rock of Ages

Earth's history is written in stone. The seemingly unremarkable rocks that pass unnoticed beneath human feet tell a fascinating story, revealing the origins and development of the Earth and the organisms that have populated it. Each rock has its own tale to tell, whether it is an igneous rock, formed by the cooling of hot magma; a sedimentary rock, created by wind and water; or a metamorphic rock, transformed by heat and pressure deep within the Earth.

Rocks reveal not just their origins but also their ages. Sedimentary rocks build up gradually in layers, or strata, with the oldest rocks in the bottom layers and the youngest rocks at the top. Fossilized organisms trapped in these sediments preserve the record of life's evolution on the planet; they also allow scientists to classify distinct geologic time periods, from the Precambrian era, which covers 90 percent of Earth's history, to the comparatively recent ice ages of the Pleistocene epoch. The age of rocks can also be determined by the rate of decay of radioactive isotopes within them. Rocks also hold a record of changes in Earth's magnetic field, giving insight into the motions of continents in the epochs before the first humans walked the Earth.

Air, earth, fire, and water wrote the elemental story of these columnar basalts in Yellowstone National Park. Formed in fire and eroded by wind and rain, these rocks record their own history.

How Are Rocks Formed?

Rocks of different ages and origins make up the crust and upper mantle of the Earth. Igneous, or "fiery," rocks, for instance, form as magma cools and becomes solid. This occurs mainly along the edges of plates and at magma-producing hot spots.

When igneous rocks appear at the Earth's surface, wind and water erode them and carry the rock fragments and other materials into the ocean. There, over time, the weight of each layer compacts the layers under it into sedimentary rock. Fossils provide information on the environment at the time and place the rocks formed.

When plate movements take these rocks deep into the Earth, high temperatures and pressures squeeze and crumple them, transforming them into metamorphic, or "changed form," rocks. These are found mainly in the subduction zones at plate boundaries.

Sedimentary layers of alternating mudstone and sandstone reveal a region's geologic history.

Where rocks are formed

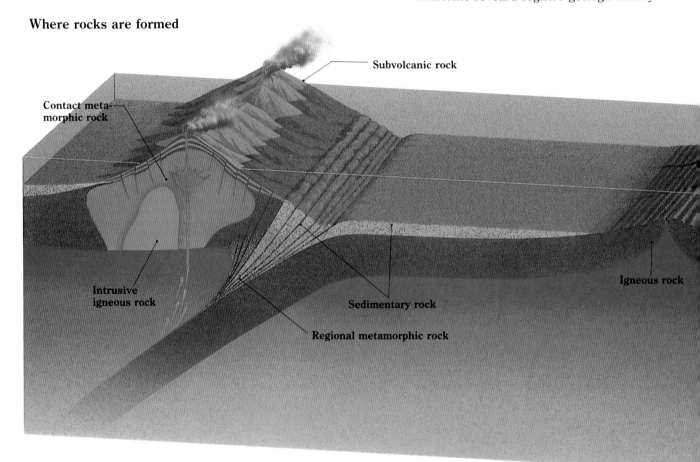

Some igneous rocks form from magma that emerges from the Earth's mantle along mid-ocean ridges and continental rift valleys, and as lava from volcanoes. Where plates converge, heat from the friction and pressure of plate subduction melts rock to create magma and, eventually, igneous rock. The high-pressure, high-temperature environment of these convergence zones also produces metamorphic rock. Sedimentary rocks may form in the ocean or in continental areas, but the specific type of rock formed depends on the local environment.

Sedimentary rocks

Wind and rain erode rocks to form clastic particles—gravel, sand, and mud—carried by rivers to the sea. There the sediments are compacted into conglomerates, sandstone, mudstone, or shale. Organic matter compacted in shallow waters or on land turns into sediments such as limestone, chert, and coal.

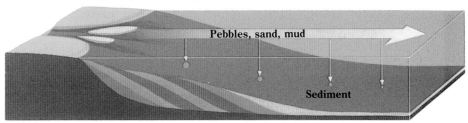

Coarse sediments of small rocks and sand sink down near a river's mouth; finer mud settles farther out.

Pebbles, sand, mud

Sediment

Eroded rock and gravel make up conglomerates.

Sandstone is made from eroded grains of sand.

Mudstone comes from mud, the finest-grained particles.

Chert is composed of microscopic marine organisms.

Igneous rocks

When molten magma cools, it becomes igneous rock. If the rock forms under the Earth's surface, intruding into other rocks, it is called intrusive. Igneous rock formed on the surface from volcanic lava or ash is called extrusive. Igneous rocks also differ by their mineral content.

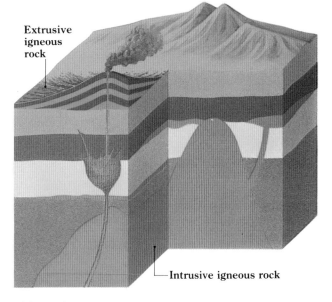

Extrusive igneous rock

Intrusive igneous rock

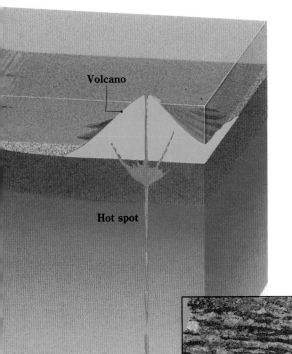

Volcano

Hot spot

Metamorphic rocks

Metamorphic rock is found in continental shields and in areas of mountain building. Contact with hot magma creates a high-temperature contact type of metamorphic rock, whereas intense pressure and little heat form a regional type.

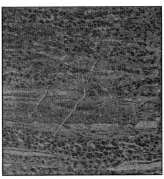

Heat and pressure create the metamorphic rock gneiss.

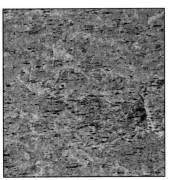

High pressures on clay-rich rock produce greenstone.

Contact with magma turns mudstone into hornfels.

87

How Is Igneous Rock Classified?

Igneous rocks, formed by the cooling and solidification of magma, are mostly made out of silica (SiO_2). However, depending on the composition of the magma, igneous rocks can differ widely in color, density, mineral composition, and texture. These characteristics identify and classify the different kinds of igneous rock.

Differences in color are mainly due to the presence of minerals, whereas differences in texture (that is, the grain size of the crystals) can be attributed to different rates of cooling by the magma. A few rocks—those that have a high content of colored minerals—are known as ultramafic; more common are dark, mafic rocks and light-colored felsic rocks.

The peridotite rock that forms the mantle is classified as ultramafic. Basalt and gabbro rocks are mafic, and granite is felsic. The oceanic crust is composed of ultramafic and mafic rocks. The continental crust contains every type of rock but is primarily composed of light-colored felsic rocks such as granite.

Nodules of peridotite form in the mantle and move upward when they are caught in rising basaltic magma.

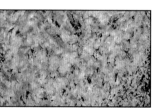

Syenite is a coarse-grained, felsic, intrusive rock containing a good deal of feldspar but only a little quartz.

Granite, commonly found in the continental crust, is a felsic intrusive rock containing minerals such as quartz.

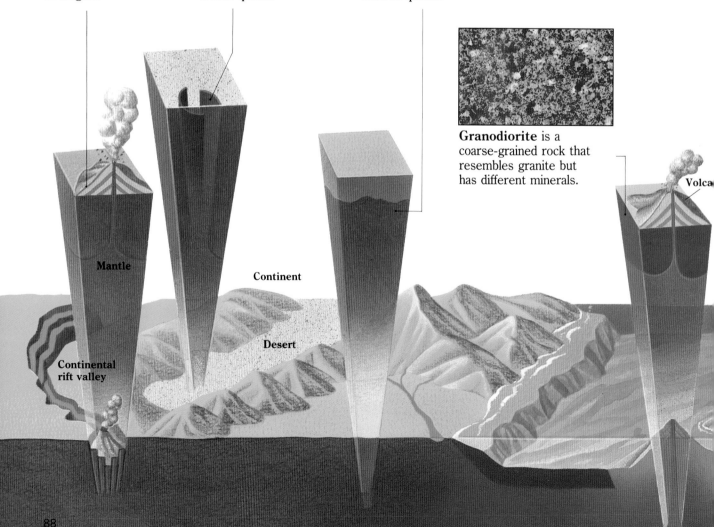

Granodiorite is a coarse-grained rock that resembles granite but has different minerals.

Volca

Mantle

Continent

Continental rift valley

Desert

Intrusive and extrusive rocks

In addition to color, igneous rocks are classified according to texture, or grain size. When magma cools slowly, mineral crystals have time to grow before the magma solidifies, and the resulting rock has a coarse grain. Since magma generally cools more slowly at greater depths, intrusive rocks are coarse grained. When magma is extruded onto the surface, it cools more rapidly and crystals have less time to grow. Rocks formed in this manner are fine grained, may have a glassy texture, and are classified as extrusive or volcanic.

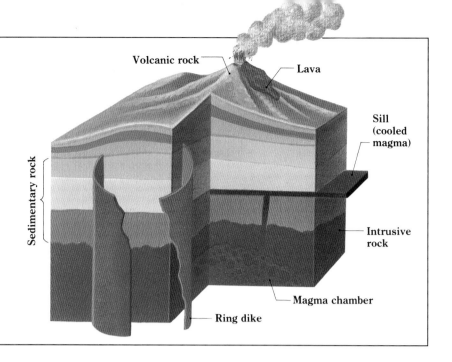

Volcanic rock

Lava

Sill (cooled magma)

Sedimentary rock

Intrusive rock

Magma chamber

Ring dike

Rhyolite is a felsic volcanic rock containing large crystals of quartz or feldspar in a glassy texture. It forms in regions of mountain building.

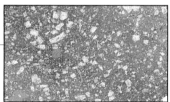

Andesite is a fine-grained intermediate volcanic rock, common in the mountain-building areas surrounding the Pacific Ocean.

Basalt *(right)* is a dark, mafic, volcanic rock with a glassy texture. It forms along mid-ocean ridges and at hot spots in the crust.

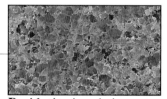

Gabbro is a dark, intrusive rock that, along with basalt, forms the oceanic crust and the lower continental crust.

Peridotite is a dark green ultramafic rock, believed to be an important part of the upper mantle.

Basalt

Gabbro

Peridotite

Volcanic island arc

Ocean trench

Mid-ocean ridge

Abyssal plain

How Are Diamonds Formed?

Diamonds are valuable because they are rare, forming only under conditions of intense heat and pressure 60 to 95 miles deep in the upper mantle. The gems are made of carbon, which in a form such as graphite is quite soft. However, when carbon is exposed to temperatures of 3,000° F. and pressures of 50,000 to 100,000 atmospheres (atm), it compresses into a hard, crystalline structure.

Diamonds occur primarily in a rock known as kimberlite, named after a South African diamond mining center. Kimberlite forms in narrow, pipelike structures that are rapidly forced to the surface by volcanic action and high gas pressures.

Diamonds in the rough sometimes have rounded edges.

Where diamonds occur

The graph at right shows the pressures and temperatures that permit diamond formation. Such conditions are found in the upper mantle.

Diamonds and graphite are both crystalline forms of carbon but are created under different conditions *(left)*. They also have a different arrangement of atoms in their crystal structures.

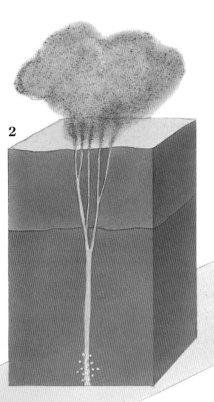

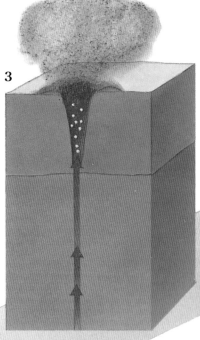

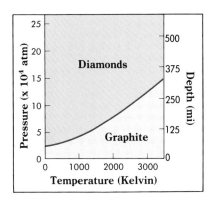

● **Kimberlite pipe formation**

According to one theory, diamonds form in volcanic pipes in the mantle (1). An explosion of gas (2) brings the kimberlite magma containing the diamonds rapidly to the surface (3), where it quickly cools (4). Many tons of kimberlite ore must be processed to recover even a few diamonds.

Model of a kimberlite pipe

A cross section of a kimberlite pipe in South Africa *(below, right)* shows rocks exposed by drilling as well as materials extruded about 70 million years ago, when the present surface layer was almost a mile deep. The bottom of the pipe may extend to the upper mantle. In addition to diamonds, the kimberlite matrix contains fragments of rock from the upper mantle that remain in virtually their original state, unaffected by heat. The presence of such rocks suggests that the kimberlite broke through surrounding rock formations and carried fragments along with it on its headlong journey to the surface.

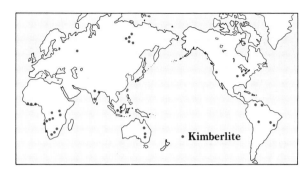

· **Kimberlite**

Diamond production

Diamond-bearing kimberlite formations are found in stable landmasses that formed more than 1 billion years ago and are unaffected by more recent mountain-building episodes.

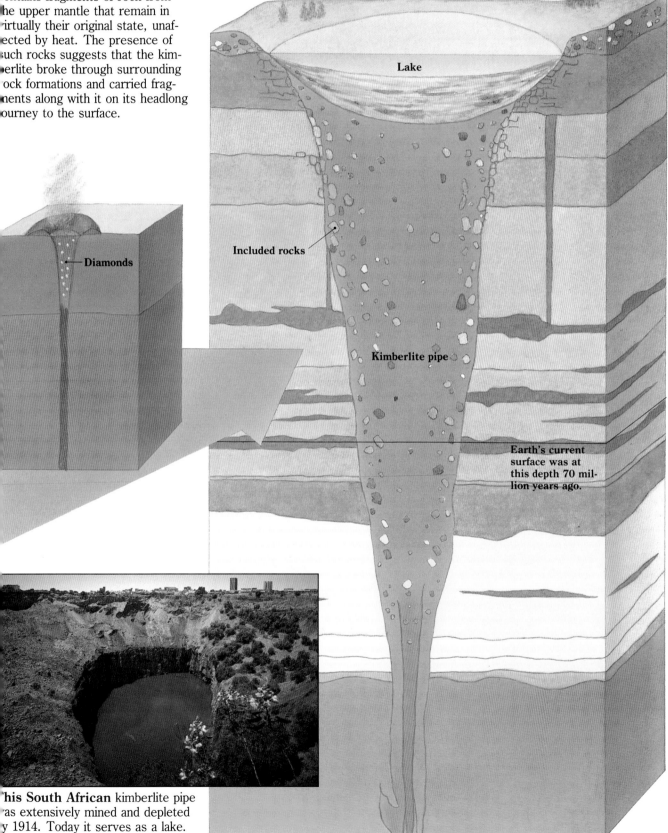

—**Diamonds**

Lake

Included rocks

Kimberlite pipe

Earth's current surface was at this depth 70 million years ago.

This South African kimberlite pipe was extensively mined and depleted by 1914. Today it serves as a lake.

What Happens to Rock over Time?

The Earth recycles its rocks. Regardless of how a rock forms, eventually the erosive forces of wind and water break it down into clastic sediments such as sand and mud. Rivers deposit the particles in the sea, where they form new sedimentary rocks.

The slow, grinding movement of the Earth's plates also recycles rocks. Both igneous rock and seabed sedimentary rock may break off, to be added to a continental landmass, or they may be dragged downward at subduction zones along the boundaries of plates. There, heat and pressure create new metamorphic rocks from the debris. Geologic upheavals may bring the metamorphic rocks back to the surface, where they once again erode. This cycle of creation and destruction unfolds over millions of years.

A river carves a path through granite, carrying particles eroded from the rock down to the sea.

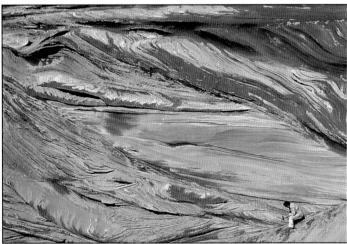

Swirling sediments of sand are preserved in layers of sandstone. Wind and water currents transport and drop particles of sand, gravel, and mud, forming new sedimentary rock.

Volcanic heat may transform seabed sediments such as mudstone into hornfels, as in these seaside cliffs.

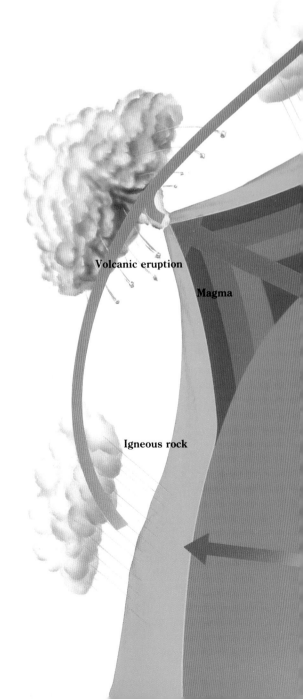

Volcanic eruption

Magma

Igneous rock

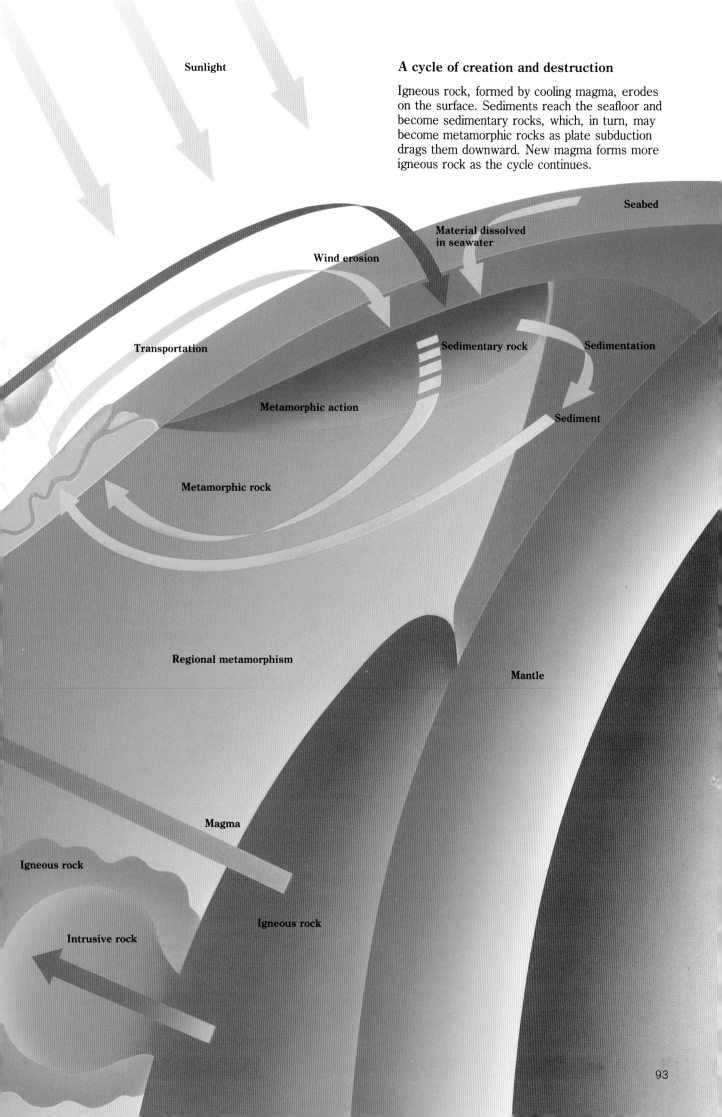

Sunlight

A cycle of creation and destruction

Igneous rock, formed by cooling magma, erodes on the surface. Sediments reach the seafloor and become sedimentary rocks, which, in turn, may become metamorphic rocks as plate subduction drags them downward. New magma forms more igneous rock as the cycle continues.

Seabed

Material dissolved in seawater

Wind erosion

Transportation

Sedimentary rock

Sedimentation

Metamorphic action

Sediment

Metamorphic rock

Regional metamorphism

Mantle

Magma

Igneous rock

Igneous rock

Intrusive rock

How Do Rocks Show Earth's History?

Since its origin 4.6 billion years ago, the Earth has evolved geologically through a repetitive cycle of deposition and erosion. Rocks preserve a record of that evolution, although it is an imperfect record, marred by gaps. Rocks also record the story of biological evolution through the fossils of organisms whose bodies are preserved in sediments. From the rocks and fossils, geologists can piece together the story of Earth's past.

A layer of uniform sediments reveals that at the time when the sediments were being deposited, environmental conditions remained constant. A change in those conditions may alter the sediments. When sediments rise to the surface, they may be eroded. If the sedimentary layers then sink again, to be covered with more sediments, the result is an unconformity, or an out-of-sequence step, in the geologic and fossil record. The principle of superposition of strata states that in series of strata, the lower strata were deposited first and the upper layers later. The same principle applies to the fossils preserved in the rock. Thus, the relative ages of the fossilized organisms can be calculated. Determining the absolute ages of rocks and fossils requires measuring the relative abundance of radioactive elements in the strata.

A window on the past is preserved in the strata exposed in the Grand Canyon in Arizona. Over millions of years, the Colorado River has carved out a chasm more than a mile deep. The strata exposed by erosion date back to the Precambrian era.

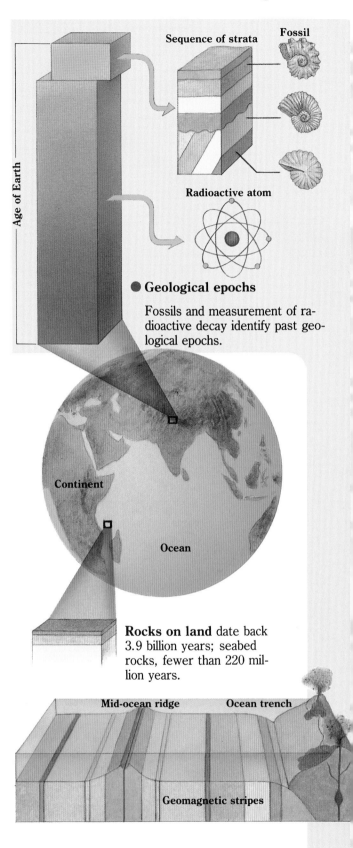

Sequence of strata

Fossil

Age of Earth

Radioactive atom

● **Geological epochs**

Fossils and measurement of radioactive decay identify past geological epochs.

Continent

Ocean

Rocks on land date back 3.9 billion years; seabed rocks, fewer than 220 million years.

Mid-ocean ridge   Ocean trench

Geomagnetic stripes

Magnetic dating

Geomagnetic indicators in seabed rocks *(pages 30-31)* form in patterns that indicate the age of the rock. They show that new rocks appear at mid-ocean ridges and are moved outward. The age of igneous rocks on the seabed therefore increases with distance from the mid-ocean ridges.

Strata deposition and Earth's history

The law of superposition of strata tells geologists the relative ages of rocks, while the composition, structure, and fossils found in the rocks reveal when and how each layer was formed. The illustrations below show how scientists can piece together the historical record by examining geological strata.

In the first step (1), gravel, sand, and mud have formed layers of sediment on the seafloor. Movement of the crust (2) tilts and lifts the sediments and exposes the strata to the forces of erosion. Subsidence (3) returns the strata to the sea, while a layer of volcanic ash creates an unconformity in the record. Decayed organic matter (4) creates more sediments until another upheaval (5) turns the swamp into an eroded desert. More changes (6) create a fertile landscape that rests on top of strata that record the region's turbulent history.

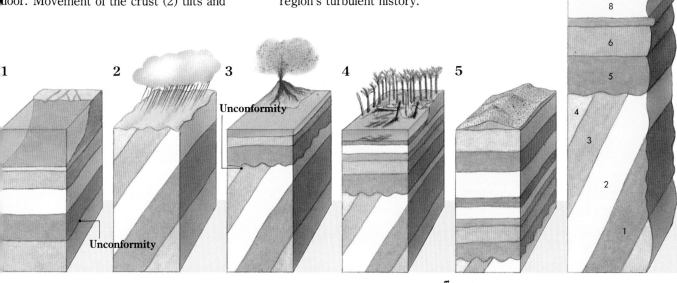

Fossils and geological dating

Each geological era can be identified by an index fossil, that is, an organism common to a particular time. The table at right shows geological periods and their index fossils.

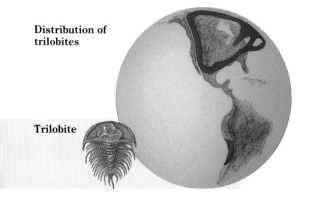

Distribution of trilobites

Trilobite

Geological periods listed below begin with the oldest, Cambrian.

		Foraminifera	Brachiopoda	Bivalvia	Nautiloids	Ammonites	Belemnites	Trilobites	Crinoidea	Sea urchins	Graptolites
	Cenozoic era										
Mesozoic era	Cretaceous										
	Jurassic										
	Triassic										
Paleozoic era	Permian										
	Carboniferous										
	Devonian										
	Silurian										
	Ordovician										
	Cambrian										

Radioactive decay and dating

Some elements have different forms, or isotopes, with different atomic weights. These isotopes decay into other elements at varying rates. For example, potassium 40 (K-40) decays into argon 40 (Ar-40). The half-life of K-40 is 1.3 billion years; that is, after 1.3 billion years, half of the K-40 present in a rock will have decayed into Ar-40. The rock's age can be determined by measuring its ratio of K-40 to Ar-40. The potassium-argon method is used to date rocks older than several thousands of years. Other isotopes used for dating include rubidium 87-strontium 87 and uranium 238-lead 206.

For younger rocks and organic matter, scientists commonly use carbon 14 (C-14), with its half-life of just 5,730 years. Carbon 14 is created when cosmic rays strike nitrogen 14 atoms in the air. Living organisms oxidize and absorb the C-14 into their bodies. As long as the organism remains alive, the ratio between the carbon isotopes C-14 and C-12 remains constant. When the organism dies, carbon 14 continues to decay and the relative abundance of the two isotopes changes. By measuring the C-14-C-12 ratio in the remains of an organism, scientists can tell how long ago it lived and died.

Uranium-lead (U-Pb) method

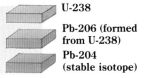

U-238

Pb-206 (formed from U-238)

Pb-204 (stable isotope)

6
Harvesting Earth's Mineral Bounty

Earth is a treasure trove of geologic riches. The entire structure of society, from microprocessors made of silicon to skyscrapers made of steel, owes its existence to minerals mined from the planet. Oil, coal, and natural gas—the fossil fuels that provide the energy needed to run civilization—are also gifts from the Earth.

Yet these gifts have limits. As world population grows, the planet's storehouse of natural resources dwindles. Alternative energy sources such as sunlight, wind, and synthetic fuels can be used to supplement and perhaps someday replace the existing supply of fossil fuels. There is no substitute, however, for minerals.

Because of this, geologists are struggling to improve their methods of finding and retrieving mineral deposits. The ocean floor, for example, harbors a wealth of minerals that lie beyond the reach of current mining technology. As geologists learn more about how these minerals formed, they get better at predicting where they will be found. This process of inquiry and discovery is explained on the pages that follow.

Since opening in 1865, Utah's Bingham mine and those around it have produced more than 10 million tons of copper, as well as 125,000 tons of gold, silver, zinc, and lead.

How Are Buried Resources Found?

Geologists looking for buried treasure—be it a coal seam, a uranium deposit, or a mother lode of gold—usually start their search with a technique called the geologic survey. Certain rock formations, they have learned, often betray the presence of a particular deposit. A mineral called kimberlite, for example, sometimes acts as a signpost for diamonds. By looking for telltale outcrops—subterranean rock formations that jut above the surface—prospectors are able to identify the most promising locations for mining.

But visible outcrops are scarce. And even when present, they provide clues to the makeup of Earth's uppermost portion only. Geologists have therefore developed less direct and far more sophisticated means of surveying. Methods that detect the minuscule variations in gravity, radioactivity, and magnetism displayed by lodes of different resources *(below)* are steadily replacing the conventional geologic survey.

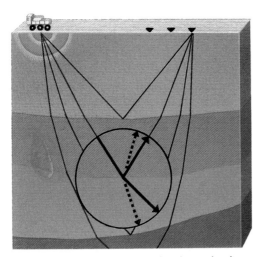

Seismic surveys. The reflecting seismic survey uses artificially generated shock waves *(above)* to probe the Earth's interior. As these waves travel from their starting point, they encounter various layers of rock. Some of the waves pass through the layer boundaries and are refracted. Others, however, reflect back toward the surface, where detectors measure their arrival times and intensities. Armed with this information, geologists can piece together cross-sectional maps, such as the one shown below, of the underlying rock.

Gravitational surveys. An ore deposit sometimes reveals its existence through gravitational effects. The density of the deposit usually differs from that of the surrounding rock, causing the gravity of one to be stronger than the other. A device called a gravimeter locates the deposit by sensing this difference.

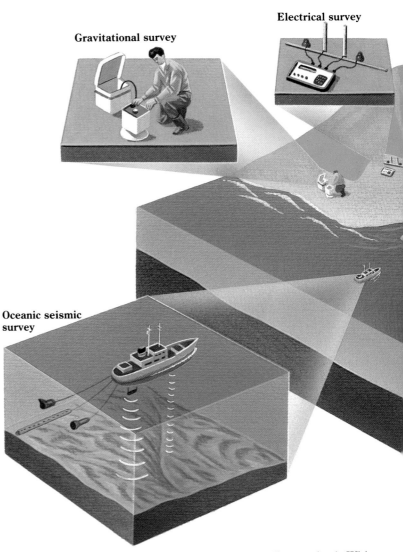

Electrical survey

Gravitational survey

Oceanic seismic survey

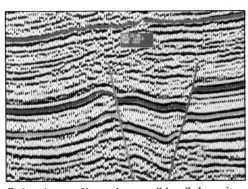

Seismic reading of a possible oil deposit

Seismic surveys can be conducted at sea as well as on land. With 71 percent of Earth's surface covered by water, the seabed and underlying rock are a potentially vast source of oil and mineral wealth.

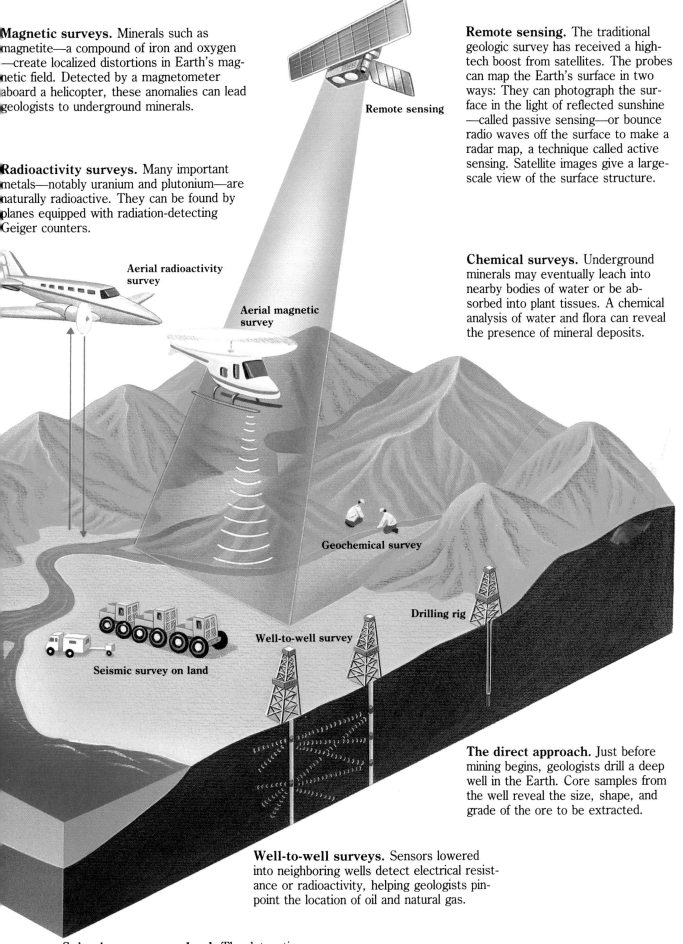

Magnetic surveys. Minerals such as magnetite—a compound of iron and oxygen—create localized distortions in Earth's magnetic field. Detected by a magnetometer aboard a helicopter, these anomalies can lead geologists to underground minerals.

Radioactivity surveys. Many important metals—notably uranium and plutonium—are naturally radioactive. They can be found by planes equipped with radiation-detecting Geiger counters.

Aerial radioactivity survey

Aerial magnetic survey

Remote sensing. The traditional geologic survey has received a high-tech boost from satellites. The probes can map the Earth's surface in two ways: They can photograph the surface in the light of reflected sunshine—called passive sensing—or bounce radio waves off the surface to make a radar map, a technique called active sensing. Satellite images give a large-scale view of the surface structure.

Remote sensing

Chemical surveys. Underground minerals may eventually leach into nearby bodies of water or be absorbed into plant tissues. A chemical analysis of water and flora can reveal the presence of mineral deposits.

Geochemical survey

Drilling rig

Well-to-well survey

Seismic survey on land

The direct approach. Just before mining begins, geologists drill a deep well in the Earth. Core samples from the well reveal the size, shape, and grade of the ore to be extracted.

Well-to-well surveys. Sensors lowered into neighboring wells detect electrical resistance or radioactivity, helping geologists pinpoint the location of oil and natural gas.

Seismic surveys on land. The detonation of an explosive charge sends shock waves through the Earth. Detectors buried far from the source gauge the intensities and travel times of the waves, which yield information about the makeup of buried rock layers.

Where Do Mineral Deposits Occur?

Plate tectonics, the process that shapes the Earth's crust, also determines where the planet's richest mineral deposits form. Earth's plates slide across, ram into, and retreat from each other, allowing molten rock to surge up into the crust. As this magma cools, minerals in the form of crystals take shape. At the same time, water seeps into the joints, where it superheats and dissolves some of the minerals. The hot water then rises and cools, and the minerals precipitate out, forming extensive bodies of ore called hydrothermal deposits.

Although most hydrothermal deposits were originally laid down along undersea plate boundaries, many of them became landlocked when these plates converged and rose up to form Earth's mountain ranges. Early miners knew, without completely understanding why, the value of prospecting in such ranges. Only recently have geologists discovered that vast mineral deposits can be found wherever oceanic plate boundaries are located. As scientists and engineers continue to refine the techniques of undersea drilling, humanity may eventually retrieve mineral riches from the ocean that far outstrip those mined on land.

Black ore, a commonplace hydrothermal deposit, is rich in sulfides of zinc, lead, and copper.

Beryl, containing beryllium and aluminum, crystallizes out of magma that wells up from Earth's interior.

A key part of Earth's interior, sulfur forms at sites of tectonic activity, often crystallizing from volcanic gases.

Rhodochrosite, another typical hydrothermal deposit, contains large amounts of manganese.

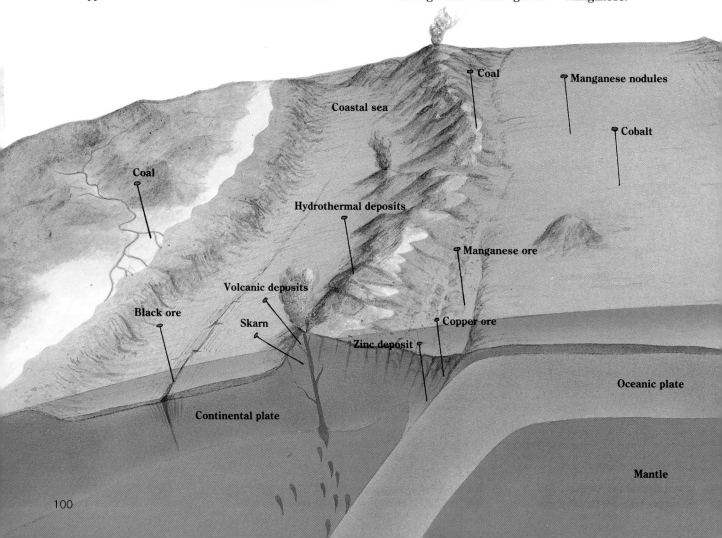

From sea to land. The top photograph at right shows an outcropping of limestone, a sedimentary rock that forms in warm, shallow waters from the accumulation of dead shellfish. Over millions of years, this deposit was pushed upward as converging continental plates rose to form the Himalayas. The mountain of rock salt at bottom right formed when shifting plates isolated a salt-water sea; the seawater then evaporated, and its salt precipitated out.

Gold, a rare metal found in its pure state, is brought to the surface by hot water from deep within the Earth.

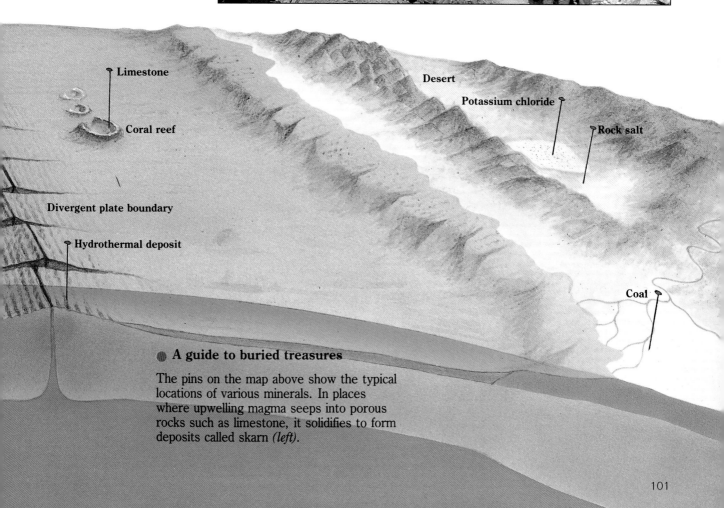

Limestone

Coral reef

Divergent plate boundary

Hydrothermal deposit

Desert

Potassium chloride

Rock salt

Coal

A guide to buried treasures

The pins on the map above show the typical locations of various minerals. In places where upwelling magma seeps into porous rocks such as limestone, it solidifies to form deposits called skarn *(left)*.

How Do Oil and Natural Gas Form?

The Earth's reserves of oil and natural gas are the legacy of plankton, algae, and other sea creatures that settled to the ocean floor millions of years ago. As ocean sediments accumulated atop these remains, they were driven deep underground and eventually decomposed into fossil fuels—the liquid and gaseous hydrocarbon molecules that can be burned for energy. In many cases, continental drift moved the rocks containing these deposits onto dry land.

The conditions required for the formation of oil and natural gas make large deposits relatively scarce. The temperature of a deposit, for example, must not be too high. The overlying rock must also be fairly dense; if not, the deposit would seep to the surface and evaporate.

Oil vapors are burned off at Ghawar, Saudi Arabia, the world's largest oil field.

Growth of a fossil fuel

Organic sediments · Sandstone · Mudstone · Mudstone and organic material · Oil-bearing rock

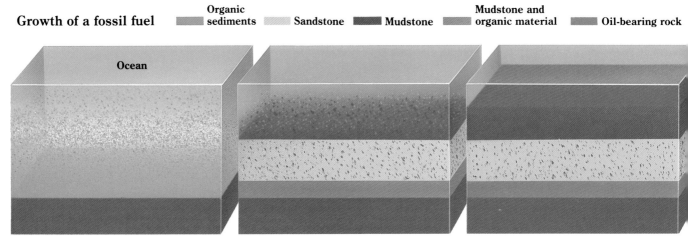

1. In stage one of fossil-fuel formation, dead algae and plankton sink to the bottom of a body of water.

2. Sedimentary materials such as mud and sand cover the organic deposits; bacteria break them down.

3. Bacterial and chemical reactions turn the bottom organic layer into oil and gas, which seeps into rock above.

A planet rich in petroleum

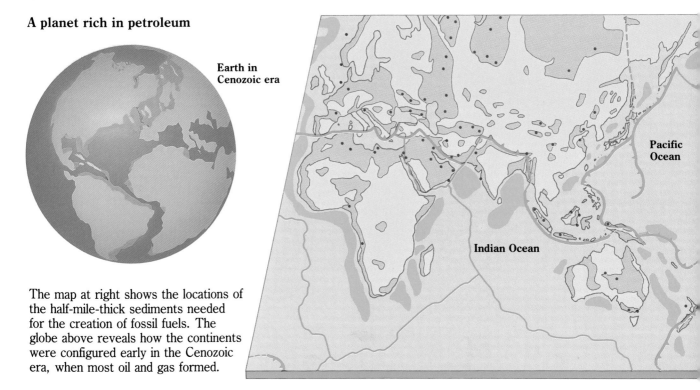

Earth in Cenozoic era

Pacific Ocean

Indian Ocean

The map at right shows the locations of the half-mile-thick sediments needed for the creation of fossil fuels. The globe above reveals how the continents were configured early in the Cenozoic era, when most oil and gas formed.

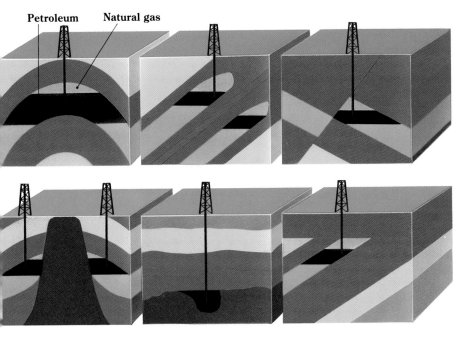

Petroleum   Natural gas

Six mixes of oil and rock

Shown at left are some typical patterns of petroleum distribution in layers of rock. Although mudstone may contain sizable amounts of oil and gas, it is not sufficiently porous for the fuels to accumulate in large, tappable pools. Rocks such as limestone and sandstone, however, have large pores; when oil reaches these "reservoir rocks," the liquid is easier to recover. Natural gas, being much lighter than oil, seeps to the top of the reservoir-rock layer.

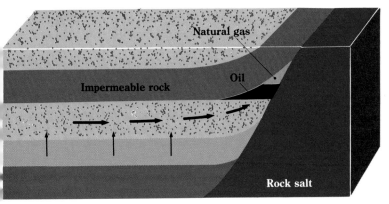

Natural gas

Impermeable rock

Oil

Rock salt

4. Rising through sandstone and other porous rocks, the oil and gas eventually reach an impermeable layer of dense rock. The fluids collect in large deposits below this layer.

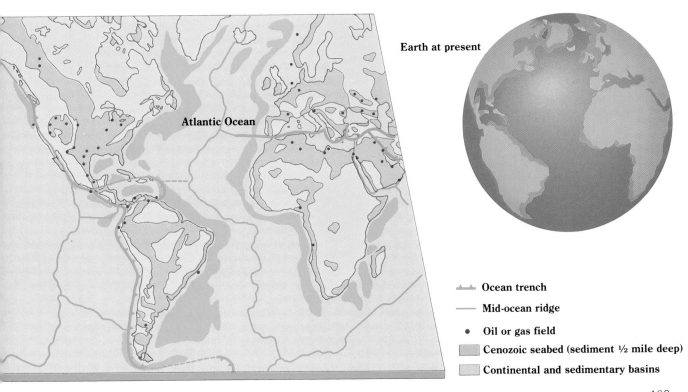

Atlantic Ocean

Earth at present

⬤⬤⬤ Ocean trench

—— Mid-ocean ridge

• Oil or gas field

▨ Cenozoic seabed (sediment ½ mile deep)

▨ Continental and sedimentary basins

How Is Coal Created?

Like oil and natural gas, coal is a fossil fuel created by the decay of organic matter. Unlike its liquid and gaseous counterparts, however, coal is a solid; it therefore requires a different set of conditions to form.

Most of the coal mined today got its start in the Carboniferous period some 300 million years ago. During this time, the remains of giant ferns and other plants accumulated in swamps and along rivers, where they were eventually smothered by sediments. Deprived of air, the remains decomposed into a soft, mossy substance called peat. As the peat sank deeper into the Earth, increasing pressure and heat began to drive away its hydrogen, oxygen, and nitrogen molecules. Ultimately, nothing was left but hard, carbon-rich masses of coal.

Geologists classify coal by its carbon content, which determines how much heat the coal will give off when burned. Lignite contains the smallest amount of carbon and is the least useful. Bituminous coal, with more carbon, is more valuable. The most precious coal is hard, shiny anthracite, with more than 98 percent carbon.

Coal in the Carboniferous period

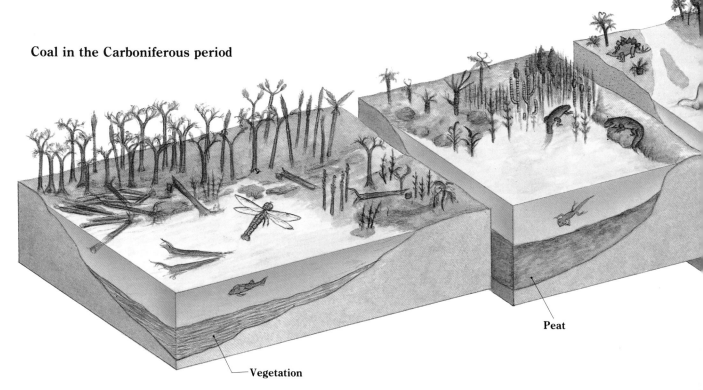

Peat

Vegetation

Under great heat and pressure, plant remains laid down during the Carboniferous period undergo a 300-million-year transformation into coal. As illustrated in the above sequence, the organic matter first turns into peat, then lignite, bituminous coal, and finally anthracite.

Earth contains about 8.5 trillion tons of extractable coal, only a few percent of which will have been mined by the end of the 20th century. As shown on the map at right, about two-thirds of the planet's known coal reserves lie in the United States, Russia, and China.

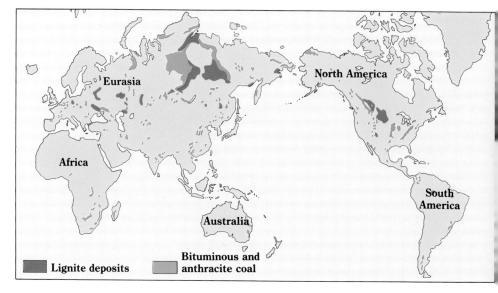

North America

Eurasia

Africa

Australia

South America

Lignite deposits

Bituminous and anthracite coal

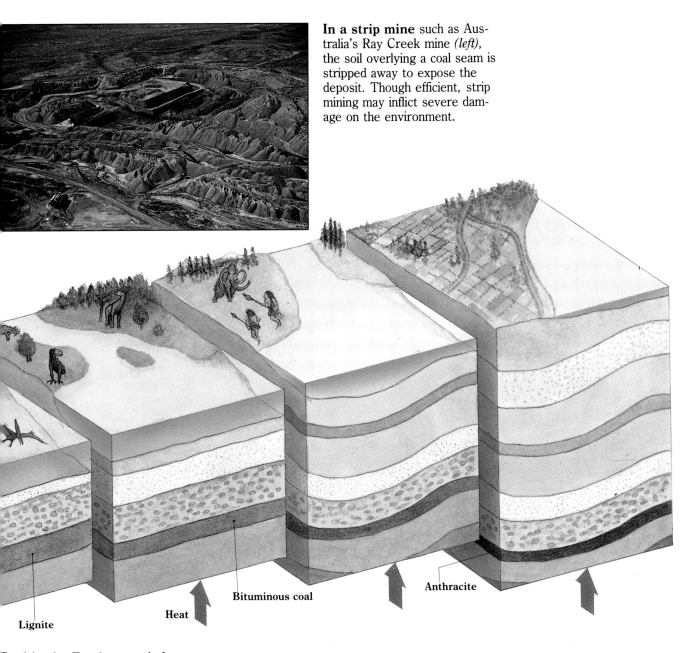

In a strip mine such as Australia's Ray Creek mine *(left)*, the soil overlying a coal seam is stripped away to expose the deposit. Though efficient, strip mining may inflict severe damage on the environment.

Lignite

Heat

Bituminous coal

Anthracite

Coal in the Tertiary period

Extreme heat hastens the conversion of organic matter into coal. This was the case in Japan *(below)*, where plant remains laid down as recently as the Tertiary period—a mere 58 million years ago—formed most of the country's coal.

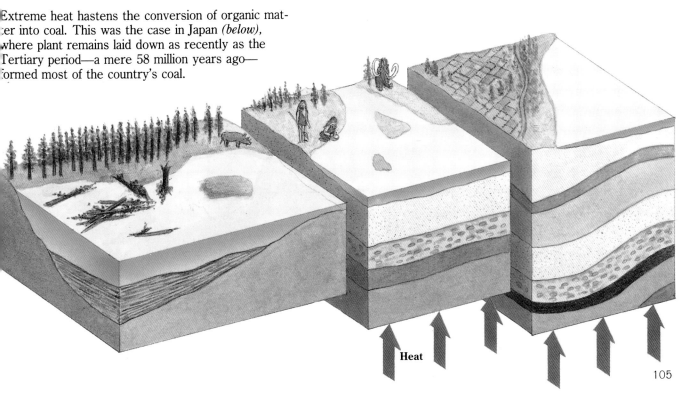

Heat

What Are Hydrothermal Deposits?

In the late 1970s oceanographers discovered evidence that vast mineral deposits, teeming with plant and animal life, exist beneath the sea. Located at mid-ocean ridges, these deposits take shape when two continental plates retreat from each other. This creates a number of gaps, which are plugged by upwelling magma. The gaps also fill with seawater, which heats up and becomes saturated with chemicals. The hot seawater then rises and cools, whereupon its dissolved chemicals precipitate out as minerals and sink to the seabed. These minerals are called hydrothermal deposits.

Because they are so rich in nutrients, hydrothermal deposits support colonies of plants and animals. They also give rise to black smokers—miniature volcanoes that shoot hot, mineral-rich water through vents in the solidified magma.

▲ **Monitored by** a submersible, a black smoker spews out mineral-laden seawater.

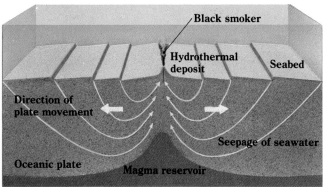

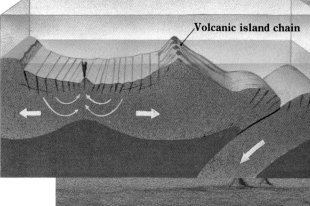

Hydrothermal deposits form along the boundary where oceanic plates diverge *(above)*. The gap between plates fills with chemical-laden magma as well as seawater, which dissolves the chemicals and deposits them as minerals on the ocean floor.

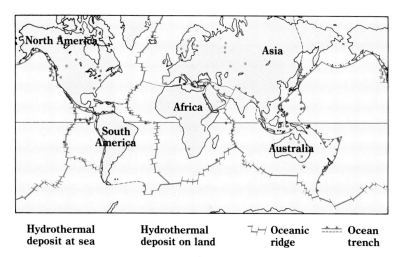

| Hydrothermal deposit at sea | Hydrothermal deposit on land | ⊐⊢ Oceanic ridge | ⩬ Ocean trench |

The above map shows the location of hydrothermal deposits that cluster near mid-ocean ridges in the Atlantic and Pacific oceans and in the Red Sea. As the continents move, hydrothermal deposits often become landlocked.

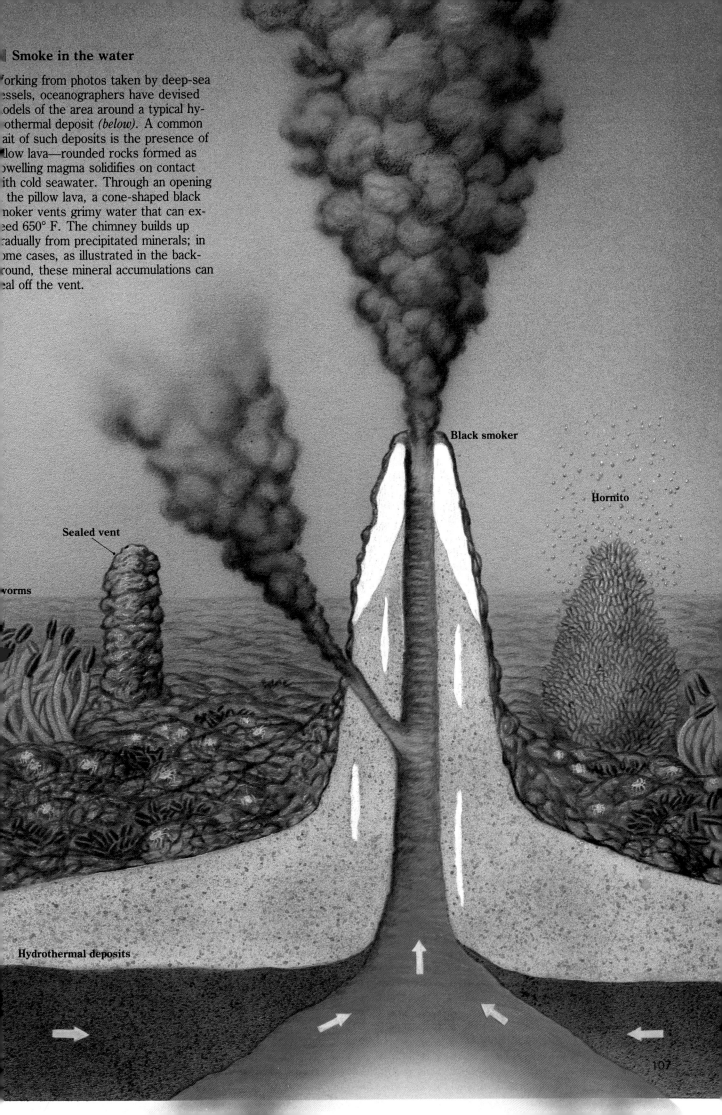

Smoke in the water

Working from photos taken by deep-sea vessels, oceanographers have devised models of the area around a typical hydrothermal deposit *(below)*. A common trait of such deposits is the presence of pillow lava—rounded rocks formed as upwelling magma solidifies on contact with cold seawater. Through an opening in the pillow lava, a cone-shaped black smoker vents grimy water that can exceed 650° F. The chimney builds up gradually from precipitated minerals; in some cases, as illustrated in the background, these mineral accumulations can seal off the vent.

Black smoker

Hornito

Sealed vent

worms

Hydrothermal deposits

7

The Oceans: Sculptors of the Planet

Had Earth been named for its surface appearance, it might be called "Oceanus" today. Seen from space, the planet shines a vivid blue, thanks to the seas and oceans that blanket nearly three-quarters of its expanse. In these waters originated the world's first life forms.

Life on Earth has evolved dramatically since then, but it still depends on the oceans. In addition to serving as an abundant source of food, the oceans govern the interplay of land, atmosphere, and water that shapes the world's climate. The ultimate source and repository of rainfall, the oceans help moderate planetary temperatures. They also cleanse the air: Organisms such as blue-green algae absorb carbon dioxide and release oxygen.

Once thought limitless, the oceans are now properly seen as vast but finite, precious but imperiled. Pollution and overfishing have reduced their biological diversity. With life on Earth so closely linked to the sea, humanity has a vital interest in protecting the oceans from further abuse.

A Hawaiian breaker crashes to shore in a classic curl. By the time it roars to this dramatic finale, the wave may have traveled thousands of miles across the Pacific Ocean.

How Were the Oceans Formed?

The history of the oceans is also the history of the Earth. When the young planet was still a stew of bubbling magma, carbon dioxide and water vapor began to rise and collect above it. These gases—plus others that escaped when planetesimals smashed into Earth—wrapped the globe in a soupy, primordial atmosphere.

Eventually, the planetesimals stopped peppering the planet, and Earth began to cool. A thin crust solidified atop the magma. With continued cooling, water vapor in the atmosphere began to condense, and torrential rains poured down up-on the Earth for tens of millions of years.

Monumental flooding ensued. Runoff from the storms flowed in great cooling rivers across the face of the planet, carving canyons in the rock and coursing toward the lowest surface levels, where it pooled to form the planet's first ocean basins. En route, the rivers swept salt and other sediments off the land and into the seas. This is how the oceans became salty. Their shorelines were not delineated until billions of years later, when the Earth's tectonic plates sculpted the basins into their present-day shapes.

1. Four and a half billion years ago, a rocky planet had coalesced, or clumped together, out of debris in the Solar System. Missiles called planetesimals pelted Earth's barren surface, gouging craters and hurling tons of material upward.

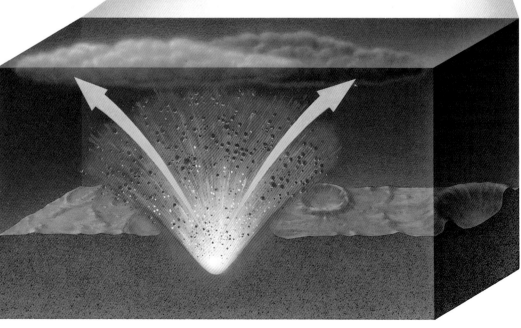

2. Each impact melted some of the surface rock, releasing gases locked inside and heating the Earth. Much of this heat was retained because the infalling debris formed a sort of insulating blanket around the planet.

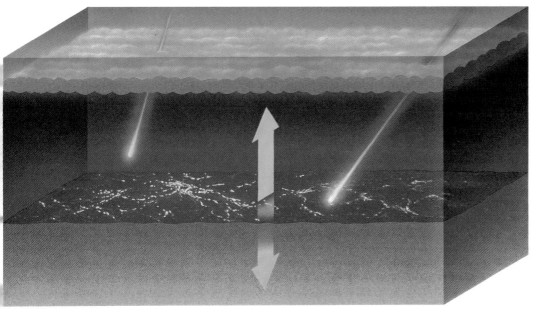

3. As the bombardment continued, the gases freed by the impacts formed a thin atmosphere. The infalling debris raised Earth's gravity, heating the planet further. This heat melted Earth's surface and vented yet more gas. Temperatures rose until lava covered the surface.

4. About three billion years ago, a cooled Earth developed a thin, rocky crust dotted with volcanoes. Cooling also caused rain to condense from the atmosphere. Storm clouds soaked the planet, and the oceans began to collect.

5. After tens of millions of years, the rains gradually ceased, and the clouds thinned to admit sunlight to the planet's surface. Finally, over eons, undersea volcanic eruptions and movement of the Earth's crust molded the ocean basins into their current forms.

What Lies beneath the Oceans?

The oceans hide a terrain rich in geologic detail. Underwater mountain ranges, plateaus, and more than 10,000 volcanoes rise from the ocean bottom. In some places, deep trenches gash the seafloor; in others, featureless plains stretch for hundreds of miles.

The submarine mountain ranges known as oceanic ridges cover almost a third of the sea bottom. Rapid seafloor spreading *(pages 30-31)* produces broad, low ridges, such as the East Pa-cific Rise; slower spreading creates more rugged ranges, such as the Mid-Atlantic Ridge. Transform faults along ridges yield canyonlike fracture zones, among them the Eltanin Fracture Zone.

Where oceanic crust sinks back into the mantle, a trench is created. The Challenger Deep in the Mariana Trench, for example, is the deepest point on Earth. The planet's tallest landform is the volcanic island of Hawaii, which soars 6 miles above the seabed.

If the world's oceans could somehow be drained, a fabulously varied landscape like the one shown at right would emerge. The dominant feature is the globe-girdling oceanic ridge system. Other points of geologic interest include arrow-straight Ninetyeast Ridge, a string of seamounts formed when the Indian plate passed over a now-extinct hot spot, and the Peru-Chile Trench, the bottom of which lies 8 miles below the peaks of the adjacent Andes. Not every facet of the seafloor is quite so dynamic, however: The abyssal plains, composed of basaltic crust and sediments from nearby continents, are the flattest areas on the planet.

Aleutian Tren
Kuril Trench
Mariana Trench
Hawaii
Ninetyeast Ridge

Charting the lands and seas

Oceans *(right, blue)* blanket 71 percent of Earth and reach an average depth of 12,200 feet. Land *(green)* covers 29 percent of the globe and has an average elevation of 2,800 feet. The deepest point is the Challenger Deep, which plunges 36,000 feet below sea level; Earth's highest peak, Mount Everest, rises 29,000 feet. The average level of the crust is 8,000 feet below sea level. Thus if the continents were bulldozed into the oceans, Earth would be covered in water 1½ miles deep.

Where Do the Continents End?

The neatly defined land-water boundaries shown on most maps do not reflect the true shapes of the continents. Each of the world's great landmasses is fringed by a continental shelf—a submerged, gradually sloping ledge that may extend the continent nearly 1,000 miles beyond its coastline. Onto this shelf, rivers deposit layers of sediment, or eroded soil and rock. Wave action then washes the sediment farther out to sea.

At the limit of the continental shelf is an abrupt drop-off, or continental slope, slashed by huge, V-shaped canyons. Beyond the continental slope, the ocean bottom descends little by little to the deeps of the abyssal plains. The continental shelf and slope—sometimes referred to collectively as the continental margin—together make up approximately one-quarter of the total area of the landmasses.

The restless Pacific Rim

The continental margin surrounding the Pacific Ocean boasts some fascinating geologic features. Ocean trenches and island arcs occur where one crustal plate meets—and plunges below—another. Guyots are flat-topped seamounts that are submerged and eroded volcanoes. Atolls form when corals growing on the submerged slopes of a guyot rise above the ocean surface, forming a ring of islands.

Continental shelf

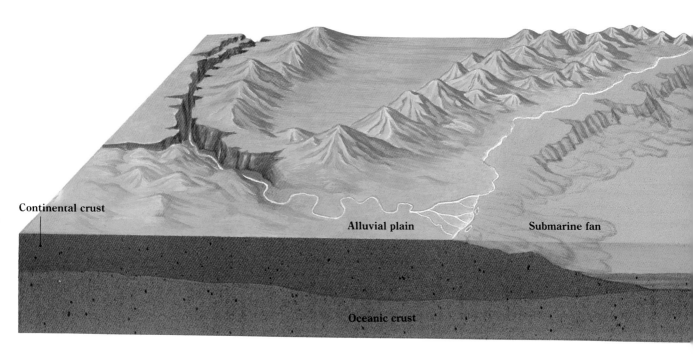

Continental crust

Alluvial plain

Submarine fan

Oceanic crust

Marginal differences

The topography of the continental shelf mirrors that of the land nearby. Off the steep, mountainous coasts rimming the Pacific Ocean, rugged, narrow shelves give way to a deep seafloor—and even deeper trenches. The gentler Atlantic coast is characterized by broad, flat shelves covered with sediment.

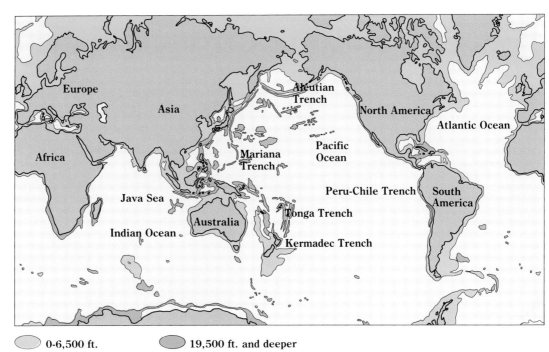

0-6,500 ft.   19,500 ft. and deeper

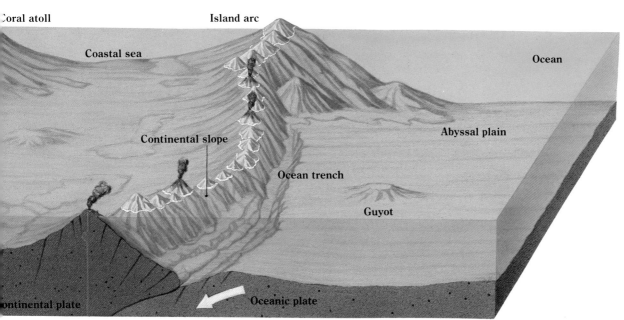

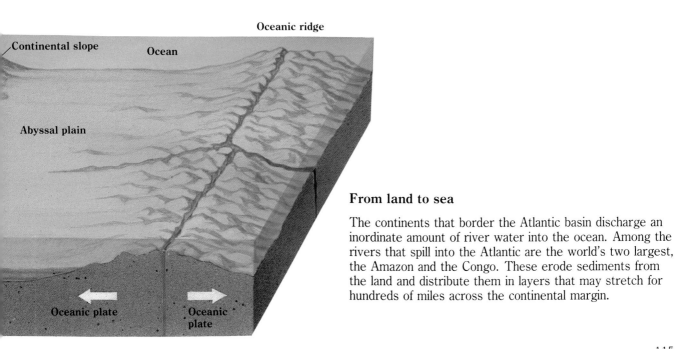

From land to sea

The continents that border the Atlantic basin discharge an inordinate amount of river water into the ocean. Among the rivers that spill into the Atlantic are the world's two largest, the Amazon and the Congo. These erode sediments from the land and distribute them in layers that may stretch for hundreds of miles across the continental margin.

How Are Bottom Currents Formed?

Bottom currents are set in motion by the interaction between the temperature of seawater and its salinity, or salt content. The colder and saltier water gets, the denser it becomes; this in turn causes the water to sink toward the ocean floor. In areas of the world's oceans where the temperature is low and the salinity is high, large volumes of surface water flow downward.

These abyssal currents, as they are called, travel along the seafloor more slowly than surface currents, but they play a larger role in circulating the world's supply of ocean water. The circulation influences not only weather patterns but the overall health of the oceans. Global warming may disrupt such currents, leading to unpredictable consequences.

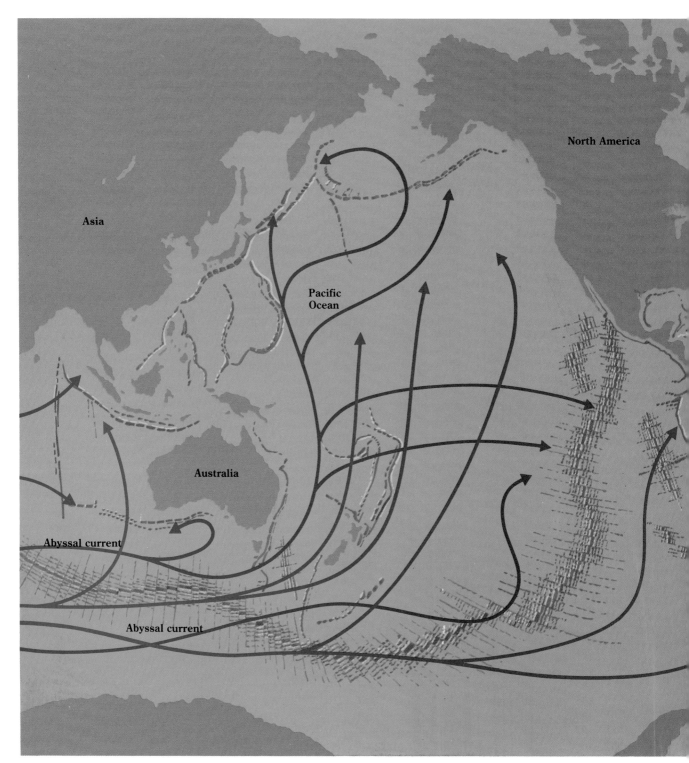

North America

Asia

Pacific
Ocean

Australia

Abyssal current

Abyssal current

Atlantic temperatures

The cutaway diagram at right reveals that a shallow layer of sun-warmed water *(dark pink)* stretches about 30° north and south of the equator. This warm layer reaches a depth of only half a mile. Below that, the water temperature drops off sharply, then stabilizes near the bottom. Currents from the polar regions have a markedly chilling effect.

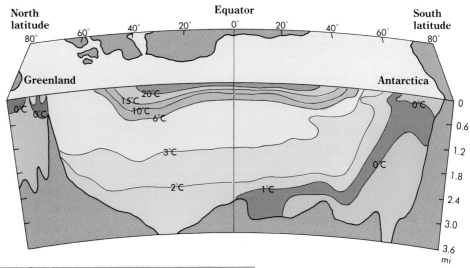

North latitude | Equator | South latitude
80° 60° 40° 20° 0° 20° 40° 60° 80°

Greenland
Antarctica

0°C 0°C
20°C
15°C
10°C 6°C
3°C
2°C 1°C
0°C

0
0.6
1.2
1.8
2.4
3.0
3.6
mi

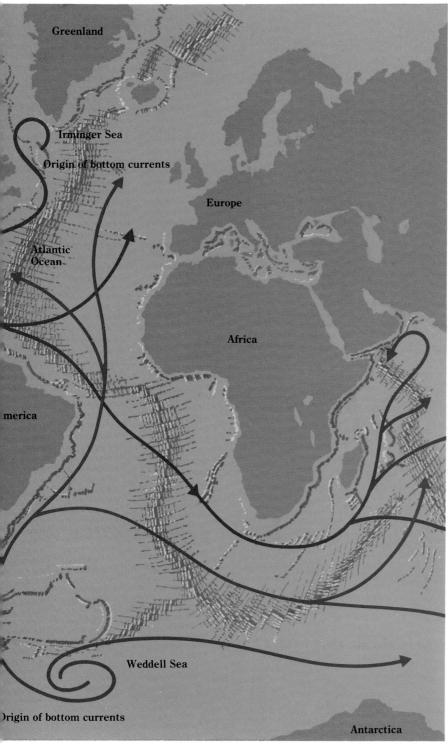

Greenland
Irminger Sea
Origin of bottom currents
Europe
Atlantic Ocean
merica
Africa
Weddell Sea
Origin of bottom currents
Antarctica

Worldwide flows

Bottom currents born in the Irminger Sea off the coast of Greenland move counterclockwise in the Atlantic Ocean before spilling into the Indian Ocean. Currents that originate in the Weddell Sea travel mainly in a circumpolar manner, extending tendrils into the Pacific and the Atlantic.

117

Why Do Surface Currents Occur?

Prevailing winds are the main source of the oceans' surface currents. The winds arise because the sun heats air near the equator, making it rise, turn toward the poles, and flow downward again. As the air rushes toward the surface, Earth's rotation deflects it in one of two directions: clockwise in the Northern Hemisphere or counterclockwise in the Southern Hemisphere.

Along the equator, this creates trade winds, which drive equatorial currents. In higher latitudes, bands of westerly winds—and currents—alternate with bands of easterlies. In the main ocean basins, surface currents trace large circles, called gyres, which carry warm tropical water toward the poles and chilly Arctic water toward the equator.

Cooking up currents

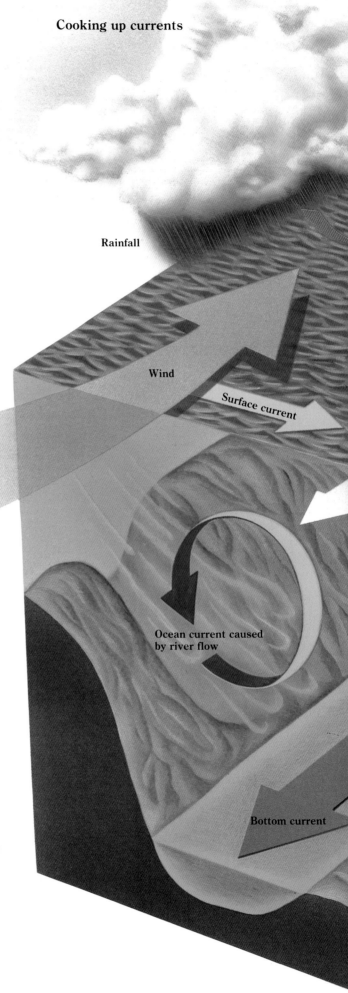

Rainfall

Wind

Surface current

Ocean current caused by river flow

Bottom current

The methodical monsoon

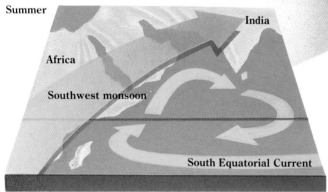

Summer

India

Africa

Southwest monsoon

South Equatorial Current

Winter

Northeast monsoon

The yearly north-south motion of the sun drastically alters atmospheric patterns and ocean currents. During summer in South Asia, prevailing winds drive surface currents clockwise, bringing heavy rains to India. In winter, winds blow from the Himalayas; currents run counterclockwise.

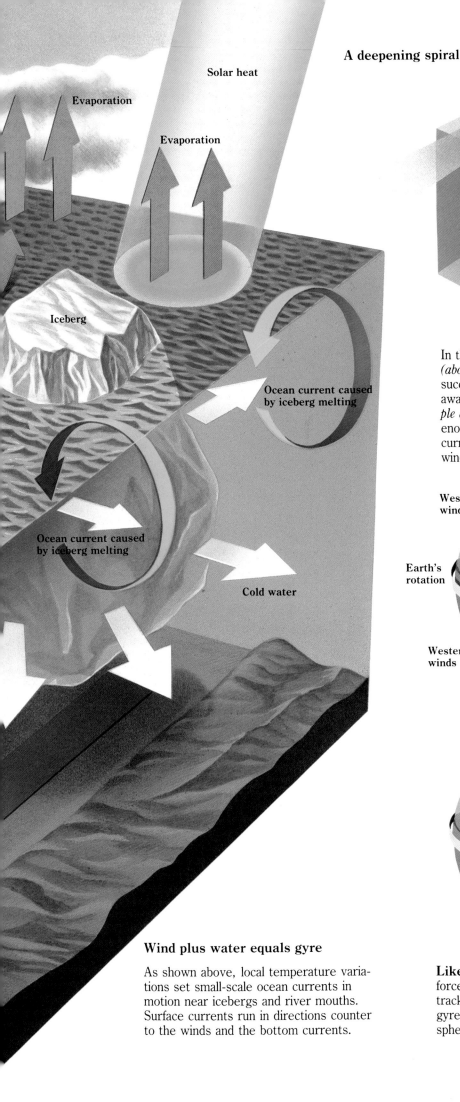

Evaporation

Solar heat

Evaporation

Iceberg

Ocean current caused by iceberg melting

Ocean current caused by iceberg melting

Cold water

A deepening spiral

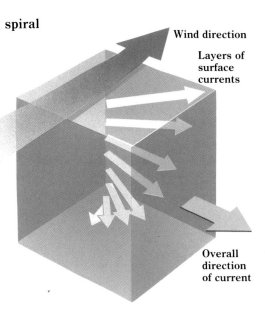

Wind direction

Layers of surface currents

Overall direction of current

In the current called the Ekman spiral *(above),* the Earth's rotation turns each successive layer of ocean water farther away from the direction of the wind *(purple arrow).* On a global scale, this phenomenon—the Coriolis effect—transforms air currents *(white arrows, below)* into trade winds and westerlies *(purple arrows).*

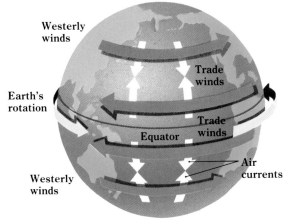

Westerly winds

Trade winds

Earth's rotation

Trade winds

Equator

Air currents

Westerly winds

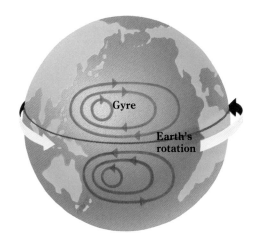

Gyre

Earth's rotation

Wind plus water equals gyre

As shown above, local temperature variations set small-scale ocean currents in motion near icebergs and river mouths. Surface currents run in directions counter to the winds and the bottom currents.

Like huge roadblocks, the continents force ocean currents to turn in their tracks. The resulting circular patterns, or gyres, flow clockwise in the Northern Hemisphere, counterclockwise in the Southern.

What Causes Warm and Cool Currents?

The atmosphere is like an engine that runs on solar energy. As shown below, radiation from the sun drives convection cells, which produce prevailing winds and ocean currents. Because the planet is curved and tilts on its axis, however, radiation warms the Earth unevenly. Equatorial surface temperatures exceed those at the poles by 75° F. Ocean currents flowing away from the equator are thus warmer than the surrounding waters; those from the poles are cooler.

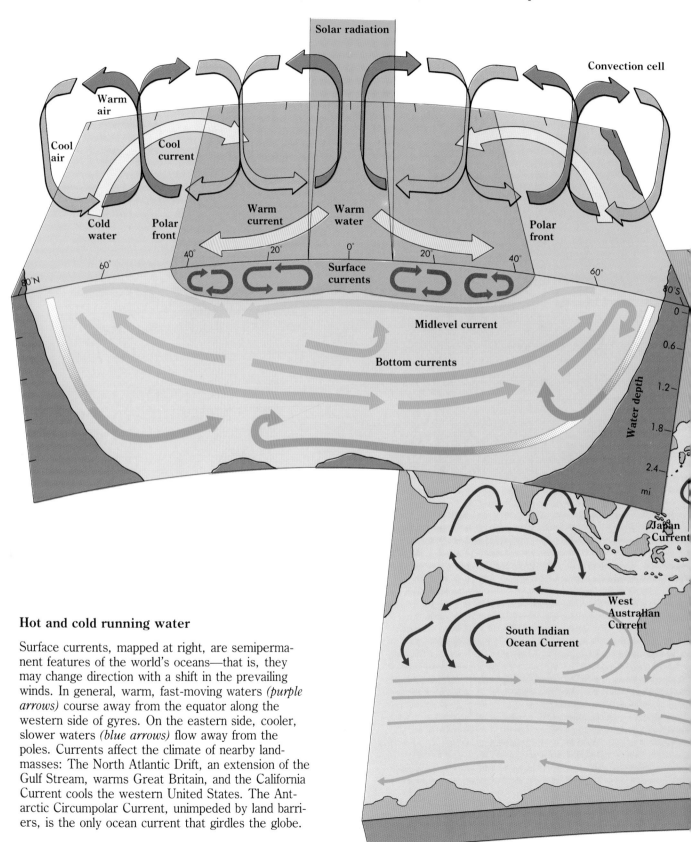

Hot and cold running water

Surface currents, mapped at right, are semipermanent features of the world's oceans—that is, they may change direction with a shift in the prevailing winds. In general, warm, fast-moving waters *(purple arrows)* course away from the equator along the western side of gyres. On the eastern side, cooler, slower waters *(blue arrows)* flow away from the poles. Currents affect the climate of nearby landmasses: The North Atlantic Drift, an extension of the Gulf Stream, warms Great Britain, and the California Current cools the western United States. The Antarctic Circumpolar Current, unimpeded by land barriers, is the only ocean current that girdles the globe.

Where cold waters rise

In certain ocean areas near continents, offshore breezes push large volumes of surface water away from land. This siphons water up from deep currents below. The phenomenon, called upwelling, runs counter to the familiar rule that cold water sinks: In this case, it rises. The bottom waters are rich in nutrients, so upwelling supplies food to microscopic organisms in the ocean's upper layers. It also exerts a moderating effect onshore; in San Francisco, for example, the cool seawater and warm air combine to produce summer fogs.

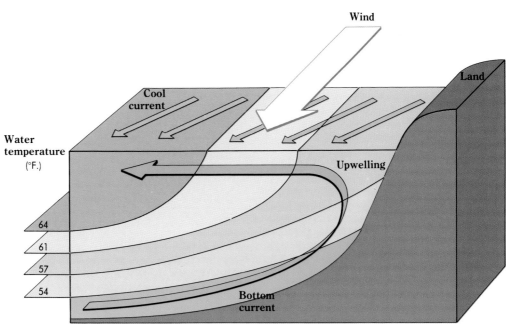

Major surface currents

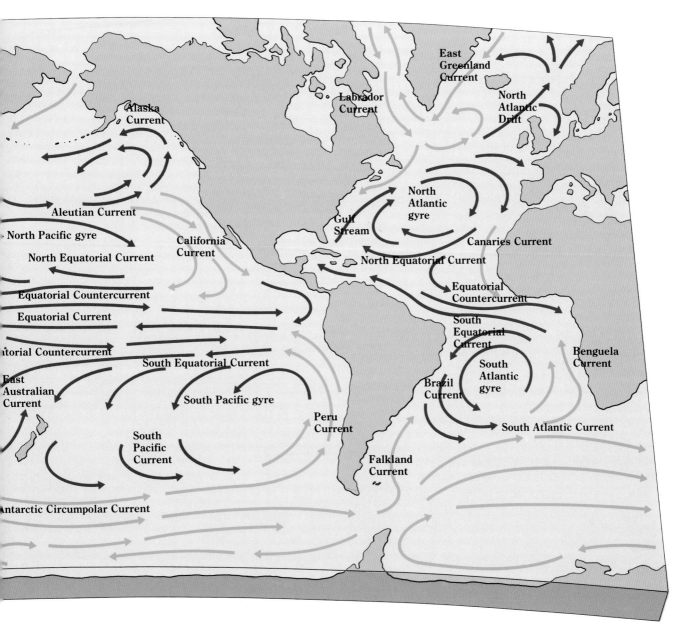

How Do Whirlpools Form?

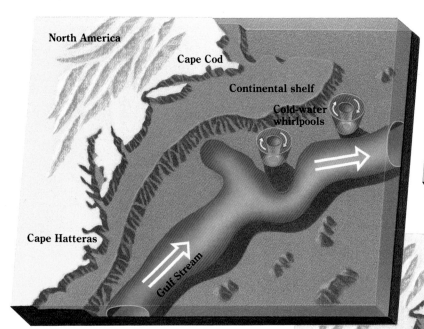

Off the east coast of the U.S., the warm Gulf Stream meets whirlpools of cold water *(above)*. As a result, the Gulf Stream is deflected eastward, and a bulge—pointing south, in this case—develops in the current.

The Gulf Stream flows from the Gulf of Mexico and east across the Atlantic.

A pronounced kink appears in the stream as the warm water flows down and around a neck of cooler water.

Ocean currents are not smooth and constant in their courses. Instead, responding to continental contours and seabed features, they twist and wriggle, fork and turn back upon themselves, or bend like the meanders of a river. When an ocean current kinks up, it often creates a whirlpool—a volume of swirling seawater as much as 100 miles in diameter.

The evolution of a whirlpool, shown on these pages, begins when a current develops a kink. Eventually, the kink becomes a closed loop. If the current then shifts, the loop breaks away, but it continues to move at the same speed—and in the same direction—as the parent current. Water at a whirlpool's edges may flow 5 feet per second.

Strong ocean currents such as the Gulf Stream, which hugs the east coast of the United States before veering northeast across the Atlantic, may change speed and even location with changes in the seasons. The Japan Current *(opposite, top),* a major feature of the North Pacific, likewise follows an ever-changing route.

Sailors take warning

In the narrow strait separating the Japanese islands of Shikoku and Awaji, strong tides and a ruggedly sculpted seafloor stir the waters into the treacherous Naruto whirlpool *(below).*

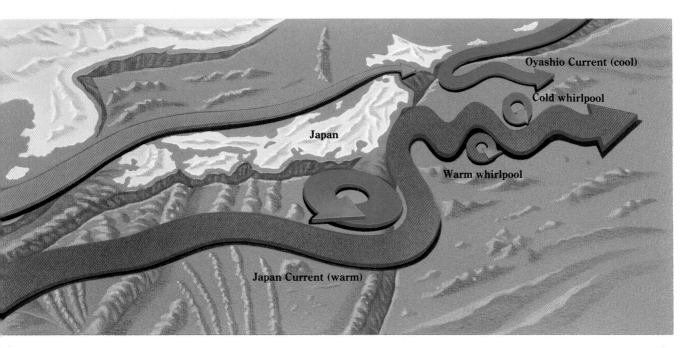

A current affair

Off Japan's east coast, two currents join to spawn a welter of whirlpools. The Japan Current, a stream of warm water that flows northeast on both sides of the Japanese archipelago, runs into the Oyashio Current, a flow of frigid water coursing south from the Arctic. The resulting whirlpools measure 120 miles across. Whirlpools spun off to the north of the Japan Current are cold; those that form to the south are warm.

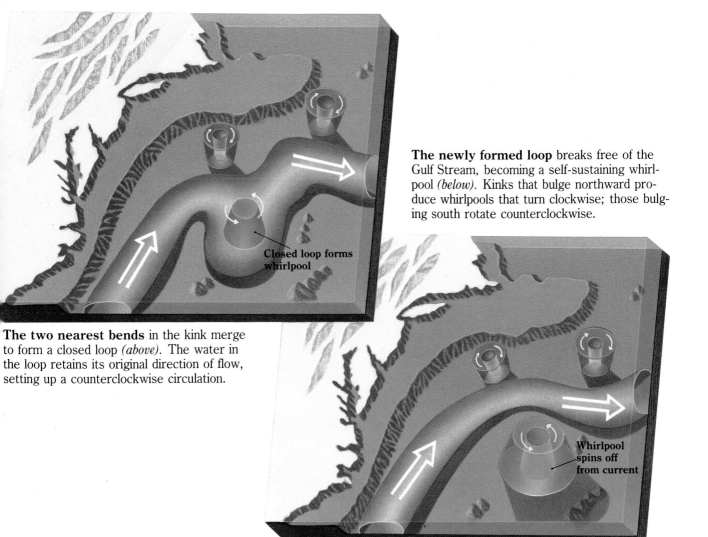

The newly formed loop breaks free of the Gulf Stream, becoming a self-sustaining whirlpool *(below)*. Kinks that bulge northward produce whirlpools that turn clockwise; those bulging south rotate counterclockwise.

Closed loop forms whirlpool

The two nearest bends in the kink merge to form a closed loop *(above)*. The water in the loop retains its original direction of flow, setting up a counterclockwise circulation.

Whirlpool spins off from current

What Causes El Niño?

Every few years, the west coast of South America is hit by drenching rains and flooding. Offshore, meanwhile, millions of fish die in seas that are both higher and warmer than usual. This event is called El Niño—idiomatic Spanish for "the Christ child"—because it often occurs around Christmas.

The force responsible for El Niño is a change in the weather patterns over the Pacific Ocean. Like a huge tub of water, the Pacific is filled with cold water at the bottom and warm water sloshing back and forth at the top. In most years, strong easterly trade winds—blowing east to west—push warm water away from the South American coast *(right)*. This causes cooler, nutrient-rich water to well up from below, feeding vast schools of fish.

In an El Niño year, by contrast, the trade winds suddenly slacken *(below),* allowing winds from the west to push warm surface water eastward. Along the South American coast, the warm water devastates fish and the creatures that feed on them, depriving the local fishing industry of its expected catch.

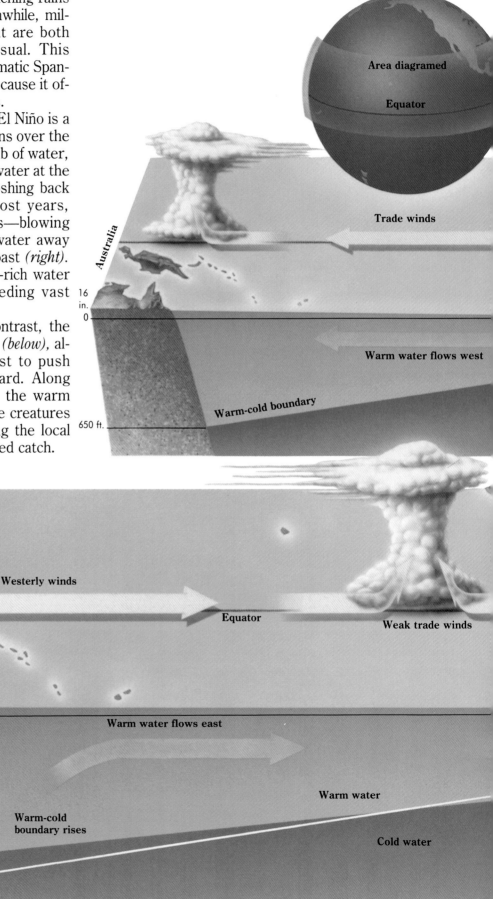

Mapping a disaster: El Niño of 1982

The maps at right show warm-water patterns during the worst El Niño in a century. In the spring of 1982, warm spots gathered off the coasts of Ecuador and Peru *(top)*. Six months later *(center)*, a 7,000-mile-long belt of warm water had piled up along the equator; sea-surface temperatures rose more than 7° F. above normal, and El Niño storms struck South America. By the next spring *(bottom)*, conditions had almost returned to normal.

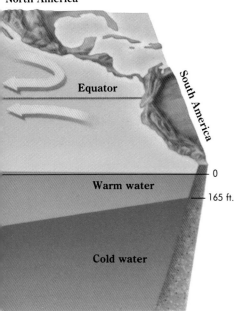

Onset of El Niño: Spring 1982

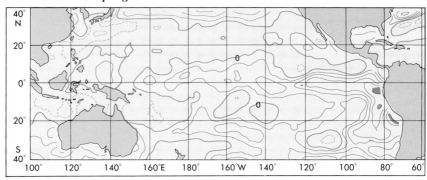

Height of El Niño: December 1982

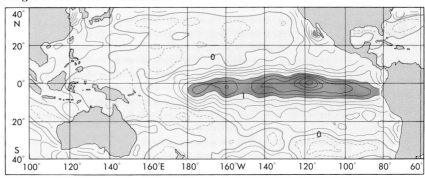

Decline of El Niño: Spring 1983

More than 2° F. above normal	0 to 2° F. above normal	0 to 2° F. below normal

Each contour line represents a temperature difference of .4° F.

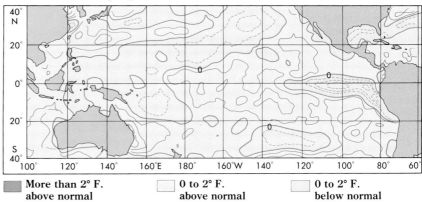

Not-so-tranquil times in the Pacific

El Niño results from changes in weather systems all across the Pacific, but its effects are most intense at the equator. Normally *(left, top illustration)*, the prevailing trade winds push warm surface water away from the Peruvian coast and toward the western Pacific. Strong trade winds also trigger life-giving monsoon rains in southern Asia. When the trade winds weaken, however, warm water and moist wind move eastward *(bottom illustration)*, and El Niño occurs. Asia suffers droughts, while rains fall on the ocean or drench the coastal deserts of Ecuador and Peru. Warm water piles up offshore, forcing the cooler water down.

How Do Waves Travel?

When wind blows steadily over an expanse of ocean, it transfers kinetic energy—that is, energy of motion—from molecules of air to molecules of water, creating waves. Though the waves appear to transport volumes of water as they travel, they actually cause the water in any given spot to revolve about a fixed center. Water particles rising to the tops of their paths form the crest of a wave; those heading downward form the trough.

In the open ocean, sets of waves from different directions tend to overlap, producing random surface patterns. Under a single, steady breeze, however, waves can march in parallel across hundreds of miles. As they near the shore, the waves break in a manner determined by the shape and slope of the beach.

Breakers crash against the base of a seaside cliff.

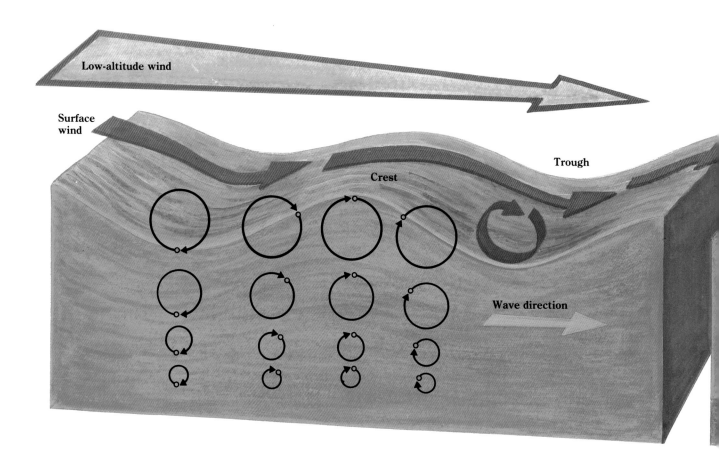

The up-and-down life of a wave

Contrary to appearances, water particles set in motion by a wave in the open ocean *(above)* trace circular rather than linear paths. Because the kinetic energy diminishes as the water deepens, the diameter of the paths shrinks with depth. Nearing shore *(above, right)*, the particles have less room to move, and their paths become elliptical.

The distance between successive crests or troughs in a series of waves is known as the wavelength. Offshore, a wave begins to "feel bottom" where the water depth is less than half its wavelength. When this happens, the water particles in the trough are overtaken by those in the crest, and the surf breaks *(above, far right)*.

Surf shaped by shoreline

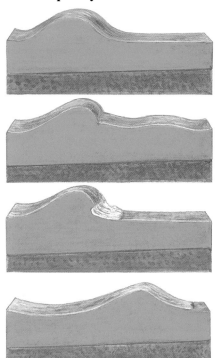

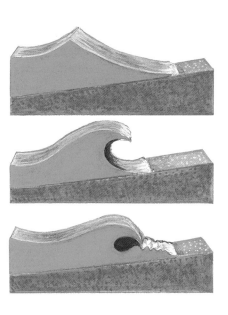

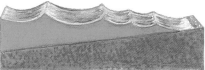

When the approach to solid land is a gently sloping sea bottom, spilling breakers result. The waves barely crest; instead, they tumble forward in a frothy cascade, losing energy as they run shoreward.

Plunging breakers take shape when a wave advances over a steeply inclined shore. Because the bottom of the wave slows down faster than the top, the wave gains height, curls forward, and smashes ashore.

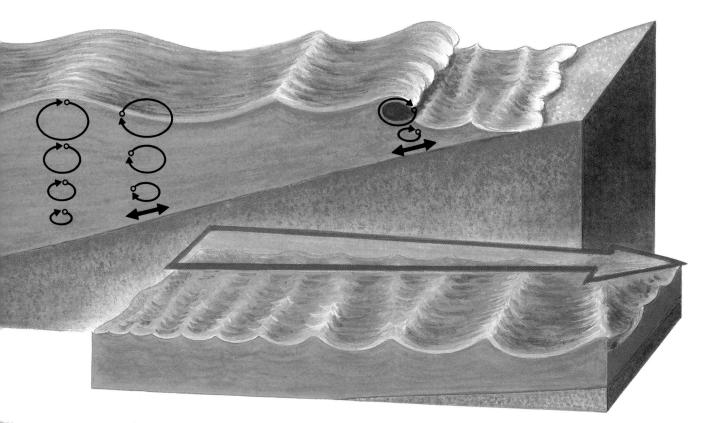

Waves=wind+time+fetch

The waves' height depends on the strength, duration, and "fetch," or travel distance, of the wind that produced them. Waves created by a constant breeze are tallest at the end of the wind's fetch.

What Are Ocean Tides?

The Sun and the Moon exert gravitational tugs on the Earth, causing the oceans to ebb and flow in daily patterns called tides. Although the Sun is much more massive than the Moon, it is also much farther away from Earth; the Sun's gravitational pull on the Earth and its oceans is therefore less than half as strong as the Moon's. The tides form slight bulges of water on opposite sides of the Earth.

As the Moon circles the Earth, the tidal bulges follow its path. If the Earth did not spin on its axis, the bulges would make a circuit every 27 days—the length of time it takes the Moon to travel once around the planet. As it is, however, the spinning Earth catches up with the bulges and passes through them. On ocean shores, this re-sults in twice-daily high and low tides, occurring about 50 minutes later each day. The difference between the height of high tide and the height of low tide is called the tidal range.

The combined pulls of the Moon and Sun typically produce a 30-inch tidal range. But tidal ranges often exceed that when the shape of a shoreline exaggerates the tides. In Nova Scotia's Bay of Fundy, the steep shore and canyonlike entrance to the bay yield a tidal range of 50 feet.

▲ **Seawater covers a rocky shore** at high tide *(above, left)* and exposes it at low tide *(right)*. Such tidal pools support a rich array of marine plants and animals.

◍ The tidal teamwork of Moon and Earth

Both lunar gravity *(green arrows, below)* and centrifugal force *(yellow arrows)* contribute to ocean tides. The two countervailing forces produce a net tidal effect that is shown by the red arrows. Centrifugal force arises from the motion of the Earth-Moon system around a common center of gravity *(bottom)*.

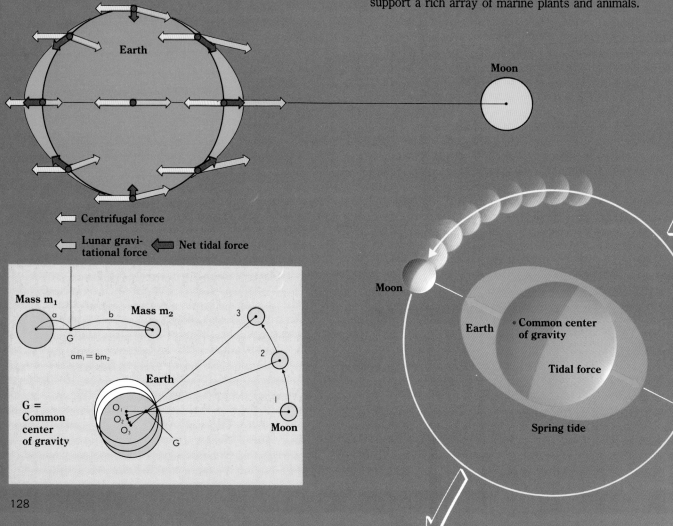

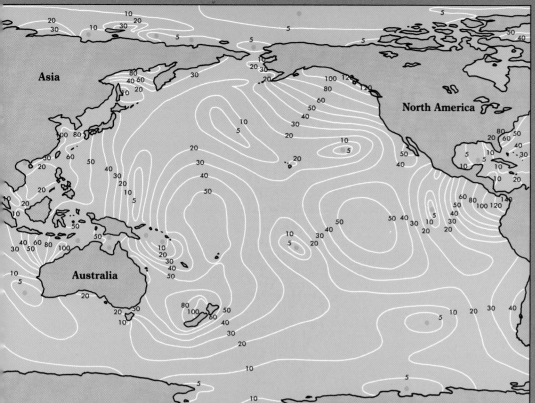

Tides in the Pacific

Tidal ranges of 1 to 1½ meters (40 to 55 inches) are common in the Pacific Ocean, especially in areas where a curved shoreline funnels rising waters. The contour lines on the map at left represent 10-centimeter (4-inch) increments in tidal range, except around the dark blue dots, where variations of 5 centimeters (2 inches) are shown. Along shorelines near the blue dots, tides are almost imperceptible.

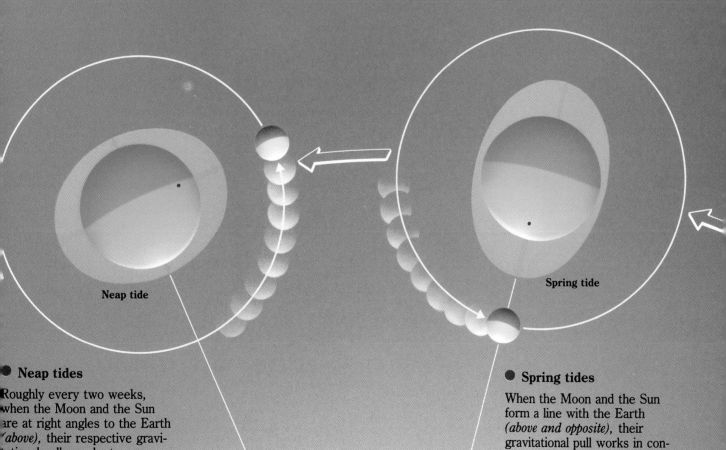

Neap tide

Spring tide

Neap tides

Roughly every two weeks, when the Moon and the Sun are at right angles to the Earth *(above)*, their respective gravitational pulls work at cross purposes; the result is weak, or neap, tides.

Spring tides

When the Moon and the Sun form a line with the Earth *(above and opposite),* their gravitational pull works in concert to produce extra-high tides called spring tides.

Sun

Why Are Storm Waves So Deadly?

Storm tides are abnormally high tides caused not only by the Moon but also by tropical storms that form over oceans. These storms—called hurricanes, cyclones, or typhoons—generate strong winds that blow high waves ahead of them toward the shore. A storm tide that hits land during a normal high tide is called a storm surge; it can top the customary tide level by 3 to 10 feet.

A hurricane may also bring ashore another, more powerful wave—a storm wave. The very low atmospheric pressure that accompanies the storm allows the water level of the ocean to rise: As the atmospheric pressure drops, the seawater directly below the storm clouds expands into a surface bulge. Moving along beneath the storm, the bulge washes ashore in a single, half-hour inundation that may exceed the normal high-tide mark by 20 feet. Though brief, the storm wave devastates everything in its path.

High winds, curved coasts, big trouble

Strong winds blowing shoreward *(purple arrow)* for several hours ahead of a hurricane push a storm tide of large waves onto land. If the coast reaches out into the ocean, as below, the waves are funneled into a narrowing cove, and the increase in sea level is exaggerated. A storm tide may reach shore 500 miles in advance of the hurricane that caused it.

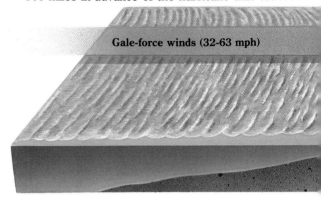

Gale-force winds (32-63 mph)

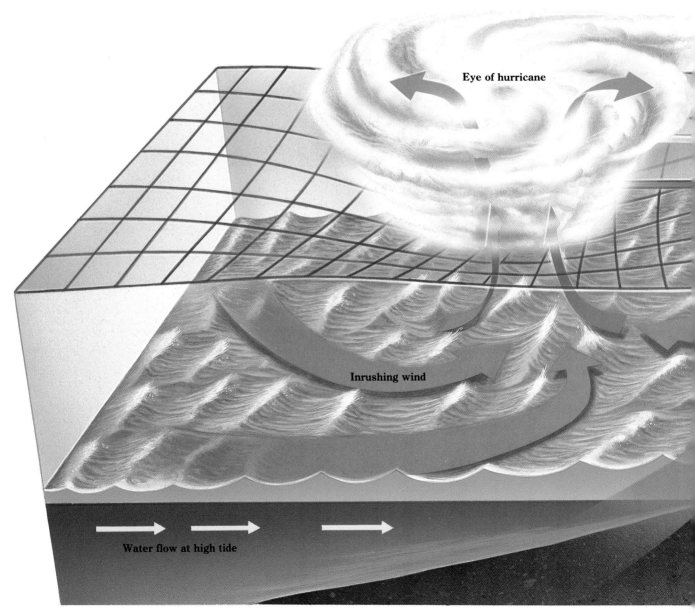

Eye of hurricane

Inrushing wind

Water flow at high tide

Stripped of its walls, a house in Galveston, Texas, forms an island amid floodwater brought inland by Hurricane Alicia in August 1983.

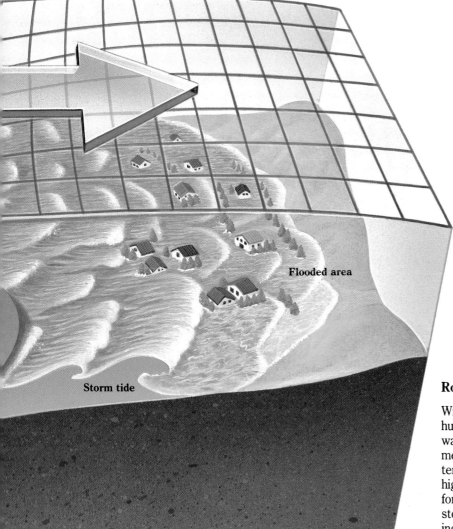

Flooded area

Storm tide

Roiling the waters

With winds spiraling 190 miles per hour, a hurricane *(left)* sucks warm, humid air upward from the surface of the ocean. Plummeting air pressure inside the storm system permits the sea level to rise, while high winds build a storm wave. Long before the hurricane smashes ashore, the storm wave may have demolished buildings along the coast.

What Is Odd about the Sargasso Sea?

A sea within an ocean, the Sargasso Sea is a slowly swirling whirlpool in the North Atlantic, about the size of the continental United States. Early sailors dreaded this strangely windless zone, fearing that their wind-powered craft would drift helplessly until all aboard died of thirst in a seaweed-clogged graveyard of ships.

Although the Sargasso's relatively still waters do in fact breed flotillas of matted ocher seaweed, modern engine-powered ships have nothing to fear. The sea's encircling currents, produced by the trade winds and westerlies *(below)*, harbor whales, eels, and many other marine creatures that spend at least part of their lives amid the sheltering weeds, in waters that remain a mild 65° F. year round.

Current events in the North Atlantic

Prevailing winds known as trade winds and westerlies ribbon the Earth *(purple arrows, left),* moving seawater in circular flows called gyres *(bottom left).* In the North Atlantic *(right),* these air-flow patterns drive the North Equatorial Current, the Gulf Stream, and the North Atlantic Drift. Earth's rotation funnels ocean water into the North Atlantic gyre, forming the calm Sargasso Sea.

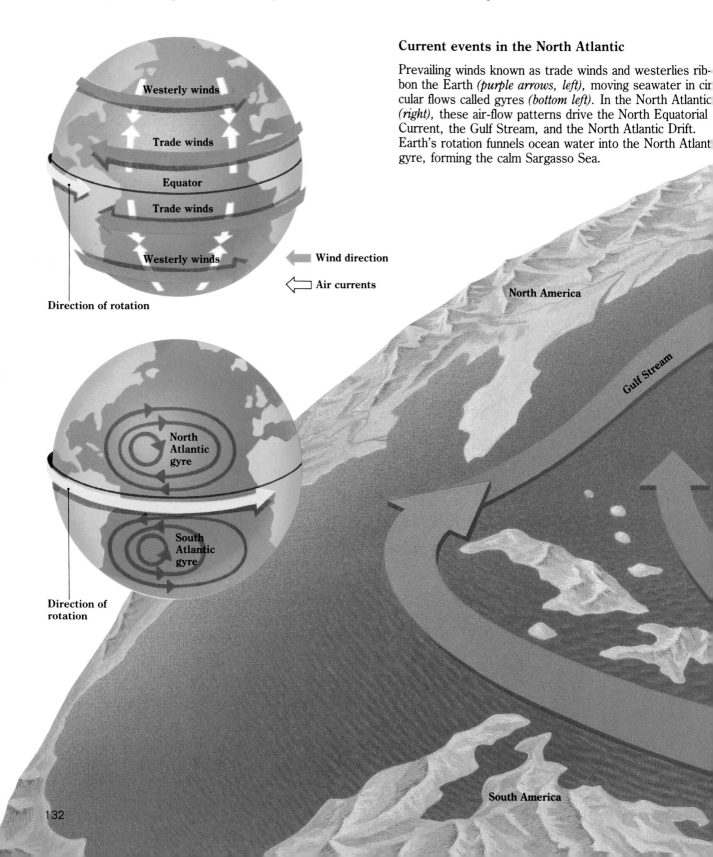

Westerly winds

Trade winds

Equator

Trade winds

Westerly winds

Direction of rotation

Wind direction

Air currents

North Atlantic gyre

South Atlantic gyre

Direction of rotation

North America

Gulf Stream

South America

An eerie Sargasso calm

The Sargasso Sea *(below),* with its perfectly clear waters, sunny skies, and unnaturally still air, gave early navigators the fearful sense that they had strayed into an enchanted realm.

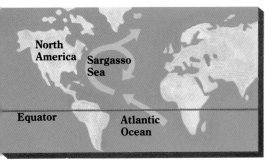

North America

Sargasso Sea

Equator

Atlantic Ocean

A cloudless patch marks the Sargasso Sea in a satellite photo. Customary high pressures over this portion of the Atlantic hold rainfall to a minimum.

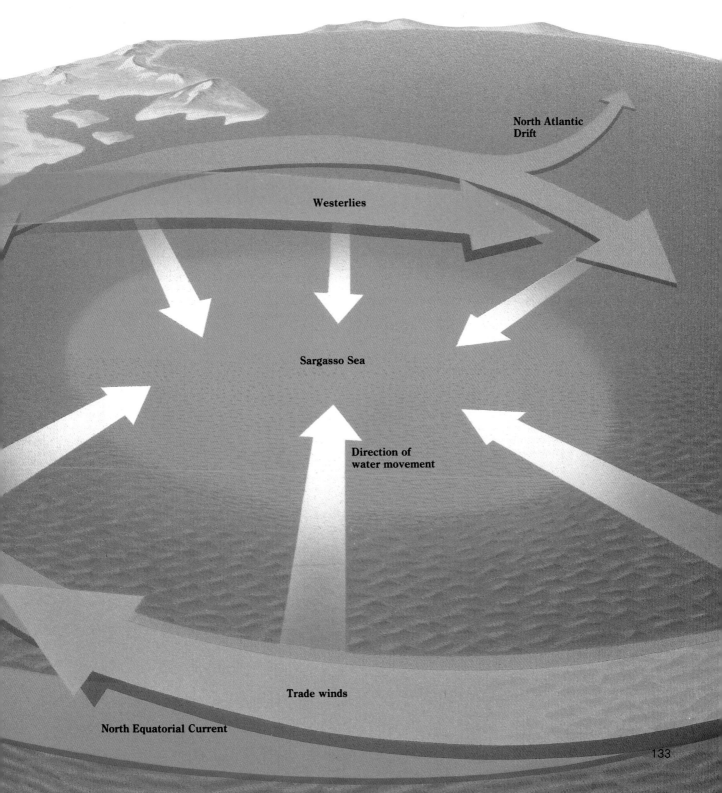

North Atlantic Drift

Westerlies

Sargasso Sea

Direction of water movement

Trade winds

North Equatorial Current

Does the Ocean Vary with Depth?

Although the oceans are in constant flux, certain features seldom change. The amount of salt in the water, for example, generally ranges from 34 to 36 percent, while temperatures rarely rise above 95° F. or fall below 32° F. Crushingly high pressures make it difficult, if not deadly, for humans to directly plumb the ocean depths. Using remotely controlled devices and instruments, however, researchers have assembled the salinity and temperature profiles illustrated on these pages.

At a certain depth in all oceans lies a sharp temperature division, called the thermocline, below which the water grows substantially colder and denser. Most of the sun's rays are absorbed by seawater in the convection layer—the upper 1,500 feet or so of the ocean, where currents and wave action ensure a steady exchange of heat. But below this, in the stratified zone that reaches all the way to the ocean bottom, the look and feel of the oceans changes dramatically. The still, cold water is lighted only dimly—or not at all. At a depth of about 3,000 feet, the colder, saltier water causes sound waves to travel more slowly than they do at the surface. But on the ocean floor, high pressures override these factors, and sound waves may actually travel faster than they do on the surface.

Seawater looks blue because it absorbs red wavelengths of sunlight and scatters blue ones.

Salinity (%)

| | 36.0 | 36.0~35.5 | 35.5~35.0 | 35.0~34.5 | 34.5~34.0 | 34.0 |

● **Salty seas**

As shown at left fo the South Pacific, saltiness varies with changes in depth and latitude. The saltiest water *(yellow)* occurs in subtropical zones, where the sun's heat evaporates water, increasing salinity. The orang areas show where rivers or melting glaciers add fresh water, reducing salinity. Below 6,500 feet, evaporation and mixing cease to be factors and salt levels average 35 percent *(purple)*.

Depth in feet: 0, 1,600, 3,200, 6,500, 10,000, 13,000, 16,500, 20,000

Latitude: 70°S, 60°, 50°, 40°, 30°, 20°, 10°, 0°, 10°, 20°, 30°N

More than one sea level

Most oceans have a distinct vertical structure, as seen in this cross section of the Pacific. At the top, winds and water currents churn the convection zone. About 1,500 feet down is the beginning of the stratified zone, a region dominated by cold, slow-moving masses of water. The top layer of the stratified zone stretches to 4,500 feet and is fed by polar deep currents. Between 4,500 and 10,000 feet, the flow of water reverses. Below 10,000 feet, frigid bottom-level water sits in perpetual dark.

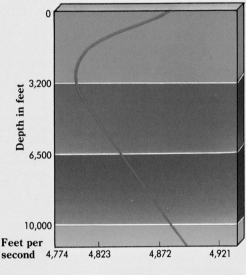

Light absorption

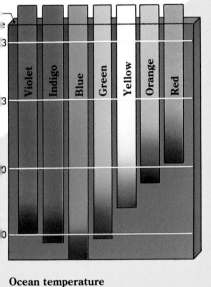

Speed of sound in ocean

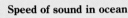

● An underwater filter

Seawater absorbs sunlight according to depth *(bar chart, far left)*. Red wavelengths are taken up within the first 30 feet; blue wavelengths penetrate more than 10 times that far.

● Sound speeds

Sound waves move faster in the upper 1,500 feet of the ocean *(near left)* because of higher temperatures. Between that depth and about 5,000 feet, sound waves slow down. Below 5,000 feet, high pressure makes the waves move faster.

Ocean temperature

28°C | 28~22°C | 22~16°C | 16~10°C | 10~8°C | 8~6°C
6~4°C | 4~2°C | 2~1°C | 1~0°C | 0°C

The icy depths

Ocean waters are warmest in a band straddling the equator. There, the layer of warm water above the thermocline is at its thickest. Sea ice, or frozen seawater, is common near the poles. Below the thermocline, temperatures vary only slightly, from about 10° C. to 2° C. (50° F. to 36° F.).

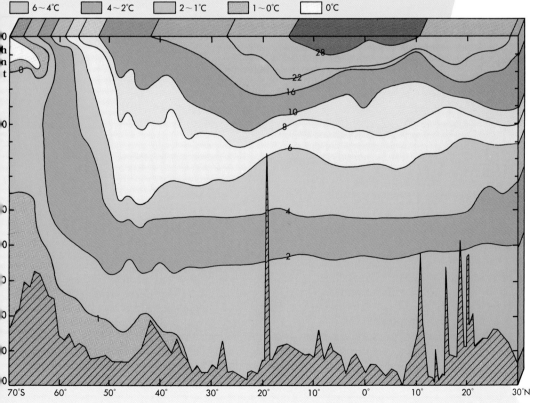

135

Why Do Satellites Scan the Oceans?

From as high as 22,300 miles above the Earth, satellites train their electronic eyes on the world's seas. Their mission is to monitor the motions of the oceans, and they perform it with an accuracy impossible to achieve on land.

Satellites observe the flow rates of ocean currents. They discern large-scale wave patterns, as well as minute shifts in ocean elevations. They also provide fixes—that is, accurate navigational readings—for ships anywhere on the globe. Instruments aboard some satellites can even make precise maps of the seafloor.

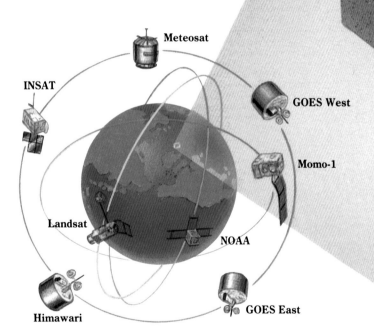

Pack ice

Meteosat

INSAT

GOES West

Landsat

Momo-1

Landsat

NOAA

Himawari

GOES East

Using sensors that collect data in the visible, infrared, and thermal parts of the spectrum, Landsat scans the entire planet every 16 days.

World weather watch

Weather satellites such as Himawari, which hovers in a high, geostationary orbit, and NOAA, which travels in a low, polar orbit, record visible and infrared light reflected from Earth. These readings help scientists predict the planet's long-range climate.

High-flying eyes in the skies

The use of satellites or aircraft to gather information about the Earth is known as remote sensing. Infrared detectors like those aboard Landsat reveal the relative temperatures of land and sea. Laser beams bounced off the ground help map elevations. Microwaves generated and received by satellites measure water vapor in the air, providing clues about hurricanes and other complex weather systems. Even changes in the speed of an orbiting satellite can identify areas where Earth's gravity is greater than normal.

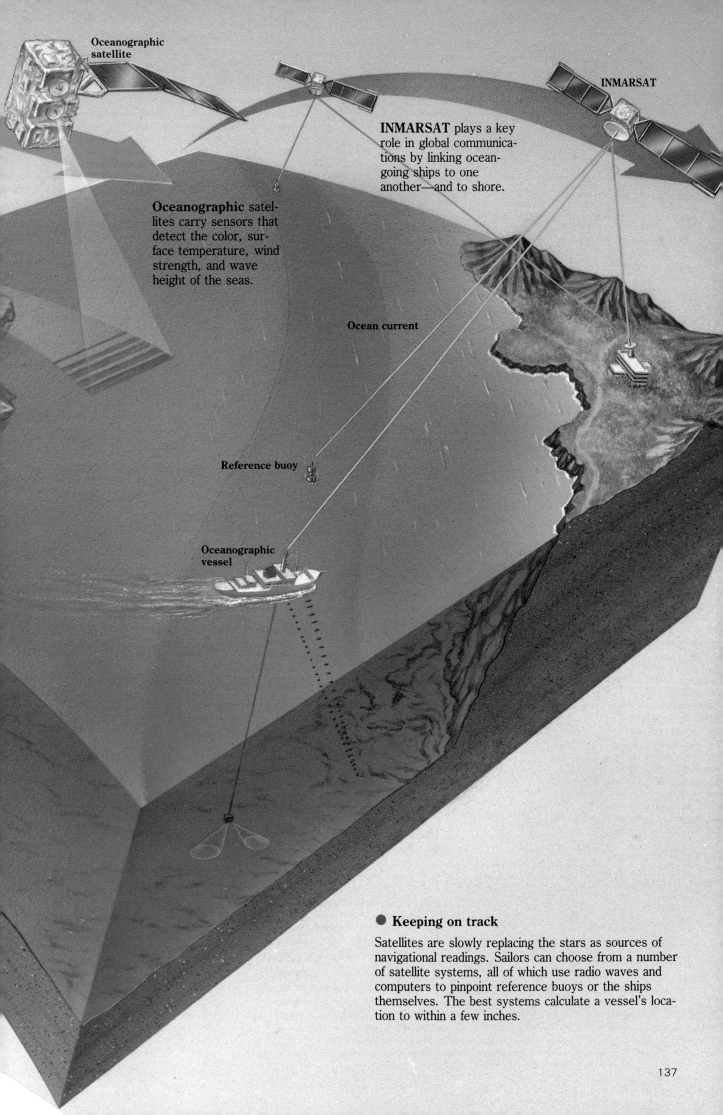

Oceanographic satellite

INMARSAT

INMARSAT plays a key role in global communications by linking ocean-going ships to one another—and to shore.

Oceanographic satellites carry sensors that detect the color, surface temperature, wind strength, and wave height of the seas.

Ocean current

Reference buoy

Oceanographic vessel

● **Keeping on track**

Satellites are slowly replacing the stars as sources of navigational readings. Sailors can choose from a number of satellite systems, all of which use radio waves and computers to pinpoint reference buoys or the ships themselves. The best systems calculate a vessel's location to within a few inches.

What Resources Do Oceans Contain?

The chemical makeup of seawater

Seawater contains at least 80 elements. Just 11 of these elements *(below)* account for 99.9 percent of all the solids dissolved in the oceans. Chlorine and sodium—with concentrations of 19,000 and 10,500 parts per million respectively—are by far the most prevalent elements. Sulfur, magnesium, calcium, and other common elements occur in lesser concentrations.

Proportions of elements in seawater

Trace elements
Bromine
Carbon
Potassium
Calcium
Magnesium
Sulfur

Chlorine
Sodium

Harvesting uranium from the sea

Although the uranium content of seawater is minuscule—only three parts per billion—the world's oceans contain a total of 4.5 billion tons of the radioactive element. Engineers are therefore eager to refine the technology, developed in the 1950s, for recovering uranium from seawater.

The procedure involves three steps. First, the seawater is treated with the chemical titanium oxide, which absorbs any uranium. Second, hydrochloric acid is added to free the uranium, causing it to precipitate from solution. Third, the liquid is filtered through a meshlike resin. This step, called ion exchange, boosts the uranium to approximately one million times its original concentration. The uranium can then be refined for use in power plants.

Uranium extraction plant

Manganese nodule mining

With the Earth's reserves of oil, minerals, and metals slowly being depleted on land, geologists and engineers have stepped up their efforts to recover these resources from beneath the sea. As of the early 1990s, one-sixth of U.S. petroleum was being pumped from offshore oil fields, most of them located on the shallow continental shelves. By the turn of the century, mining companies may begin tapping seafloor deposits of manganese and extracting dissolved uranium from seawater. Ultimately, the oceans may become sources of minerals, energy, and even fresh water *(right)*.

Harnessing waves, tides, and temperatures

The energy available from the oceans dwarfs that produced by all the power plants on Earth. Several prototype power systems have begun tapping this potential. In thermal stations, for example, warm surface water vaporizes ammonia, which drives turbines that generate electricity. Tidal dams, like the one near St. Malo, France *(right)*, channel the sea's ebb and flow through reversible turbines. And wave stations use the motion of waves to compress air and run turbines.

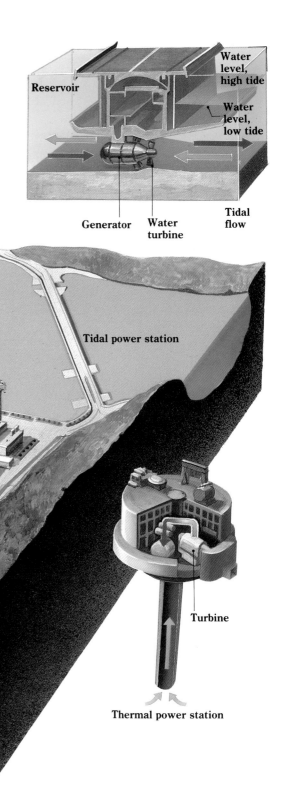

Reservoir

Water level, high tide

Water level, low tide

Generator **Water turbine** **Tidal flow**

Thermal power station

Tidal power station

Wave power station

Desalinization plant

Deep-water pumping

Turbine

Thermal power station

Seawater solutions

Many desert nations—and even the city of Santa Barbara, California—obtain their drinking water from desalinization plants, which remove salt and other dissolved substances from seawater. In a process known as reverse osmosis, the seawater is forced through a membrane that allows only pure water to pass to the other side.

What Are Manganese Nodules?

Scattered across the world's deepest seafloors are peculiar black lumps called manganese nodules. Usually no larger than potatoes, the nodules consist of up to 34 percent manganese, a metal essential for making steel. They also contain enough iron, copper, cobalt, and nickel to be classified as ores—materials that can be mined for their metal content.

Manganese nodules may blanket 20 to 50 percent of the Pacific Ocean bottom. When sliced in half, most nodules reveal a core of rock, shell, or shark's tooth, suggesting that the nodules start forming when metals dissolved in seawater adhere to a small, hard grain on the seabed.

As land-based ore deposits grow scarcer, the idea of retrieving manganese nodules becomes ever more attractive. The challenge is to devise an economical—and ecologically safe—way of scooping the nodules from the seabed and transporting them to the ocean surface 3 miles above.

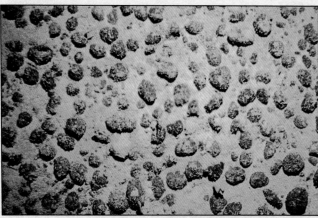

▲ **One-inch** manganese nodules litter the ocean bottom like charred potatoes.

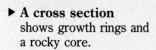

▶ **A cross section** shows growth rings and a rocky core.

● **A worldwide phenomenon**

The global distribution of manganese nodules is shown below. Discovered by researchers in the 1870s, the nodules have been found in every ocean of the world.

● **The manganese mystery**

Manganese nodules are a source of puzzlement to scientists: Where did the nodules' constituent metals come from? How did the nodules form? And why aren't the nodules buried by the sediments that constantly rain down on the ocean floor?

One theory holds that the metals originate in thermal vents that spew out mineral-laden waters, or in geologic fracture zones where the rock of the seabed is constantly being crushed. A second theory, illustrated at right, argues that microscopic plankton absorb and retain certain metals dissolved in seawater (Steps 1 and 2). When the plankton die, they settle to the ocean floor and decompose (Step 3), leaving concentrated metals behind. Bacteria then ingest this metal-rich residue (Step 4), concentrating the metals even further and forming the cores of newly created nodules. Over millions of years, as the nodules are stirred by crabs, fish, and currents (Steps 5 and 6), additional metals accrete, or accumulate, in layers around the core (Steps 7 and 8). Chemical analyses of manganese nodules have revealed that a one-inch layer may take 25 million years to accumulate.

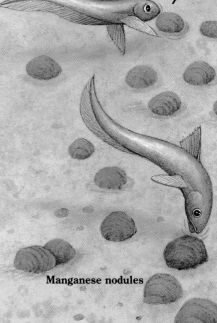

7

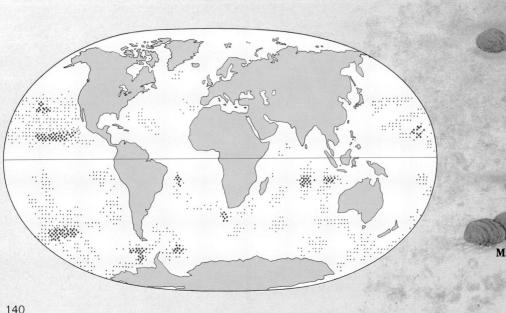

Manganese nodules

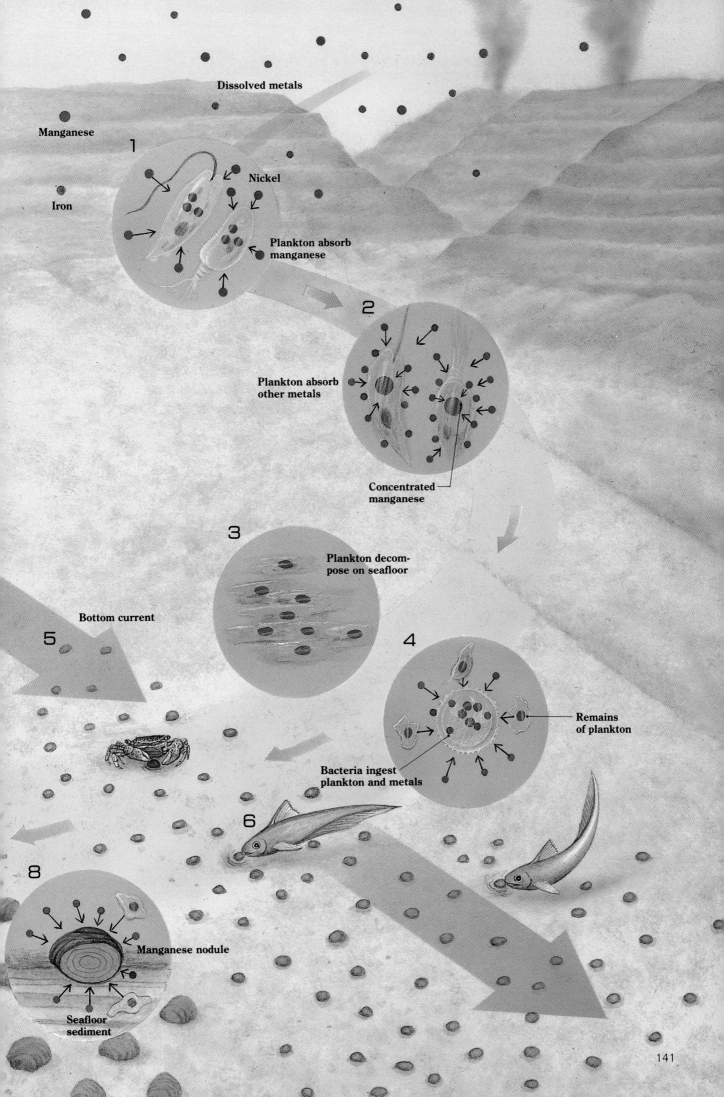

Dissolved metals

Manganese

1

Nickel

Iron

Plankton absorb
manganese

2

Plankton absorb
other metals

Concentrated
manganese

3

Plankton decom-
pose on seafloor

Bottom current

5

4

Remains
of plankton

Bacteria ingest
plankton and metals

6

8

Manganese nodule

Seafloor
sediment

Can the Oceans Be Farmed?

Raising fish or shellfish as a food source is called aquaculture. Fish are hatched in tanks or reservoirs next to or within the sea; once they reach maturity, the fish are harvested—that is, caught—and sold to markets. Experimental programs with certain overfished species, such as the tropical redfish, restore depleted populations by returning the hatchlings to the ocean. Every year, 2.2 billion salmon spawned in captivity in Japan, Russia, and the United States are released into wild rivers for their migration to the sea.

Aquaculture holds such promise that it is practiced worldwide. In Ecuador, for example, shrimp are farmed in seaside enclosures. Japan, China, and France have thriving shellfish industries, with oysters, scallops, and mussels being seeded and tended in coastal beds. In the future, floating offshore pens may be used to raise saltwater fish—as well as kelp and other seaweeds that provide food, fuel, or fertilizer.

Giant-kelp beds

Sea urchin pen

Monitoring buoy

Ocean outposts

Marine laboratories, satellites, and coastal monitoring stations provide vital support for aquaculture. To breed and raise marine species, scientists must understand the ecosystems under which the creatures flourish in the wild. The young science of marine studies will expand as aquaculture is called upon to feed the world's growing population.

Monitoring satellite

Coastal monitoring station

Artificial reef

Fish pen

143

How Might Oceans Be Used Tomorrow?

Try to imagine a world where ships dock at floating harbors, planes lift off from sea-based runways, and cities powered by the energy of the oceans rise on platforms constructed above the continental shelves. Such is the vision of futurists who predict that humanity will one day colonize the world's oceans.

The benefits of such a move, however, must be weighed against the severe ecological impact that industrialized societies have had on the oceans. Many marine species have been nearly wiped out by overfishing; others have been contaminated by oil spills. Abandoned drift nets become floating graveyards full of entangled sea creatures, while discarded plastic containers and rings ensnare or choke seals, seabirds, and other coastal animals.

Clearly, the oceans and the atmosphere are precious and finite treasures, to be husbanded with care. Indeed, they are the only things that separate planet Earth from the fate of its silent, lifeless partners in the Solar System.

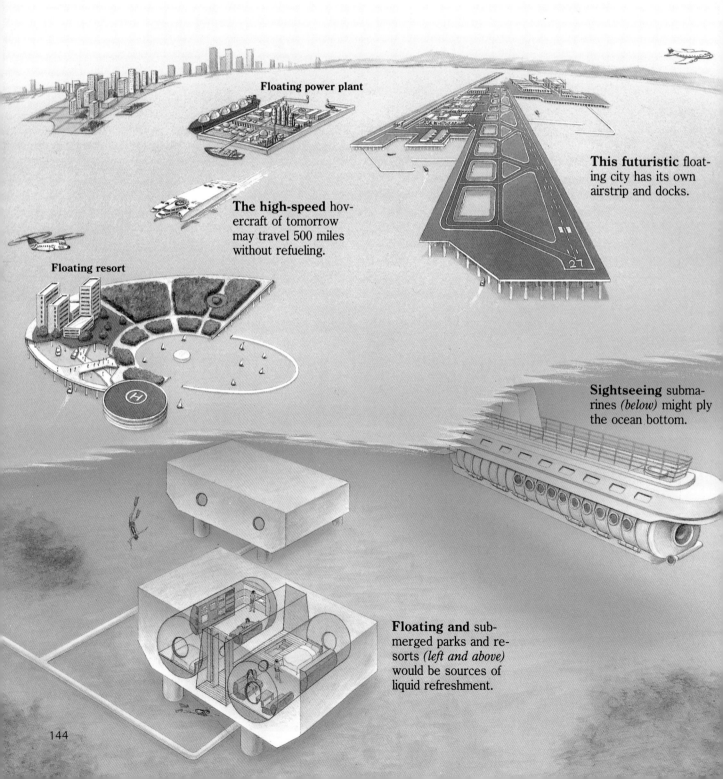

Floating power plant

This futuristic floating city has its own airstrip and docks.

The high-speed hovercraft of tomorrow may travel 500 miles without refueling.

Floating resort

Sightseeing submarines *(below)* might ply the ocean bottom.

Floating and submerged parks and resorts *(left and above)* would be sources of liquid refreshment.

Glossary

Abyssal plain: A flat, nearly featureless expanse of ocean floor, usually found at depths of 12,000 to 18,000 feet below sea level.

Alluvial fan: A fan-shaped accumulation of mud, silt, and sand deposited by a river.

Alluvial plain: A plain formed by the deposit of river sediments.

Asthenosphere: A layer in the upper mantle, lying below the lithosphere and extending to about 200 miles below the surface of the Earth. Rock in the asthenosphere—literally "sphere of weakness"—is thought to be hot, weak, and slightly fluid, allowing crustal plates to glide across it.

Basalt: A common, fine-grained, extrusive igneous rock.

Clastic: A rock or rock sediments that have been transported and deposited far from the preexisting rock from which they were derived.

Conglomerate: A sedimentary rock composed of sedimentary particles ranging in size from gravel to boulders.

Continent: A large landmass that rises above the deep ocean floor; it often includes shallow submerged areas surrounding it. *See also* Continental margin.

Continental drift: The theory that the continents ride on giant plates, which glide and move across the surface of the Earth.

Continental margin: The zone that separates a continent from the deep ocean floor. It includes the **continental shelf**—a shallow, gradually sloping area about 40 miles wide—and the **continental slope,** a steep incline that descends from the continental shelf to the deep sea bottom.

Cordillera: A group of mountain ranges, including any valleys, plains, lakes, and rivers they may encompass.

Core: The center portion of the Earth. It consists of the inner core—a solid mass of nickel and iron about 1,400 miles across—and the outer core, a fluid layer that surrounds it. The outer core lies 3,100 miles below the planet's surface.

Crust: Earth's solid, outermost layer, ranging in thickness from 5 miles beneath the oceans to 45 miles beneath mountain ranges.

Dike: A sheetlike igneous rock that has cut through a preexisting rock layer, leaving igneous rock embedded in the rock around it.

Discontinuity: A layer deep below Earth's surface that separates rock layers of different types and densities. Sudden changes in the velocity of seismic waves often indicate that the waves have crossed a discontinuity.

Earthquake: A sudden movement of plates in the Earth's crust, caused by the abrupt release of strain that has built up over time.

Epicenter: The point on the Earth's surface directly above the underground focus, or source, of an earthquake.

Extrusive rock: A type of igneous rock that formed when magma erupted onto Earth's surface and then cooled.

Fault: A fracture in Earth's crust along which movement has occurred. Motion along the fault builds up enormous strain; when the fault fails, the pent-up energy is released, causing an earthquake.

Fissure: A long, deep, narrow crack in the Earth's crust.

Focus: The underground origin of an earthquake; from the focus, seismic waves spread out in all directions through the Earth.

Gabbro: A coarse-grained, dark, intrusive igneous rock.

Geoid: The shape the Earth would have if sea level extended continuously through the continents.

Geomagnetic: A term used to describe the shape or effects of the Earth's magnetic field.

Geyser: A jet of steam and hot water that erupts periodically from a subterranean hot spring.

Gneiss: A common metamorphic rock, characterized by layers of coarse-grained quartz and feldspar.

Granite: A common, coarse-grained, light-colored, intrusive igneous rock.

Gyre: A ringlike movement of ocean currents, turning clockwise in the Northern Hemisphere and counterclockwise in the Southern Hemisphere. The Gulf Stream is part of a large gyre carrying water around the Atlantic Ocean basin.

Hot spot: A location where a stationary plume of magma rising from the mantle melts a hole in Earth's crust, producing a volcano or other igneous activity.

Igneous rock: Rock that has crystallized from a molten state. Igneous rock is one of the three major kinds of rock; the others are sedimentary rock and metamorphic rock.

Intrusive rock: A type of igneous rock that formed when hot magma cooled beneath the Earth's surface, becoming embedded in older surrounding rock.

Isochrone: A map line connecting locations at which an event occurs simultaneously; for example, points where a given seismic wave arrived at the same time.

Isostasy: A sort of geologic balancing act, in which light rocks in Earth's crust float on denser bedrock below.

Isotope: A variation of a chemical element, having the same number of protons but a different number of neutrons; radioactive isotopes are unstable, meaning their atoms disintegrate with the passage of time.

Isotopic dating: Measuring the percentages of radioactive isotopes in a rock or fossil in order to determine its age.

Lava: Hot, molten rock that reaches the surface of the Earth.

Lithosphere: The rigid outer layer of the Earth, extending down some 40 to 50 miles. The lithosphere—literally "sphere of stone"—includes the crust and the solid upper part of the mantle.

Magma: Hot, molten rock generated within the Earth.

Magnetic field: The area around an object in which a magnetic influence is felt by other objects. Earth's magnetic field, for example, is similar to that of a bar magnet; it has a north and a south pole linked by lines of varying magnetic strength and direction.

Mantle: The layer of Earth between the crust and the outer core; the mantle reaches a depth of approximately 1,800 miles.

Metal: Any of a group of chemical elements distinguished by their metallic luster, malleability, and ability to conduct heat and electricity.

Metamorphic rock: A rock whose composition, structure, or texture has been transformed without melting by heat, pressure, or chemical action. **Contact metamorphic rock** forms by coming in contact with hot magma. **Regional metamorphic rock** results from elevated pressures and temperatures. Along with igneous and sedimentary rock, metamorphic rock is one of the three major kinds of rock.

Oceanic ridge: The underwater mountain range where new oceanic crust is constantly being generated through the process of seafloor spreading.

Ocean trench: A deep, elongated depression on the ocean floor where subduction takes place.

Ore body: A continuous body of mineral material that can be economically extracted and processed for its commercial value.

Organic matter: In geology, the remains of plants or animals.

Orogeny: The creation of mountains by folding and faulting in Earth's crust.

Pangaea: The name given by German meteorologist Alfred Wegener to a hypothetical landmass from which all modern continents were formed. Pangaea, Wegener postulated, began to drift apart about 200 million years ago.

Pillow lava: Magma that has been extruded underwater and hardened in the shape of rounded pillows.

Plate tectonics: The theory that Earth's crust consists of rigid plates in constant motion. The resulting colliding, grinding, and separating motions produce intense geologic activity at the edges of the plates.

Pumice: A frothy volcanic rock that contains gas bubbles, making it extremely lightweight. Pumice often floats in water.

Radioactive element: Any chemical element whose atomic nuclei are unstable and spontaneously decay, releasing subatomic particles and heat.

Radon: A radioactive gaseous element.

Rift valley: A broad valley that forms along the line where two or more continental plates are moving apart. Rift valleys are also found on the crest of mid-ocean ridges.

Seafloor spreading: The process in which magma oozes from a mid-ocean ridge, creating new crust and causing the ocean bottom to spread outward on both sides of the ridge.

Seamount: A submerged mountain that rises more than 3,000 feet above the ocean floor.

Sediment: Tiny particles of mineral, rock, or organic matter that have been moved by wind, water, or ice and deposited on the Earth's surface.

Sedimentary rock: Rock formed from sediments that have been compacted and cemented together. The other two major rock types are igneous rock and metamorphic rock.

Seismic tomography: A computer technique that converts seismic-wave readings into detailed images showing the three-dimensional internal structure of the Earth.

Seismic waves: The form taken by energy released in an earthquake. Seismic waves travel through the body of the planet or along its surface. **Compressional waves**—also called **P waves** or **primary waves**—travel the fastest, compressing and expanding rock they pass through. **Shear waves**—also called **S waves** or **secondary waves**—travel more slowly, shaking the rock they pass through. **Surface waves,** the slowest type of all, travel along the Earth's surface.

Seismograph: An instrument that records the amount of ground movement produced by an earthquake.

Shield: A large, stable segment of older igneous and metamorphic rock that has a shieldlike shape and is surrounded by younger sedimentary rock. Shields are characteristic of stable continental interiors.

Stratum: A single, distinct layer of sedimentary rock.

Subduction: The geologic process by which one of Earth's crustal plates slides beneath another.

Tectonic plate: A rigid portion of the Earth's crust and upper mantle that moves slowly across the top of the asthenosphere.

Temblor: An earthquake.

Terrane: An area of Earth's crust in which a certain formation or group of rocks predominates.

Transform fault: A fault that cuts across an oceanic ridge, producing a **fracture zone;** if a transform fault cuts the edge of a continent (as does the San Andreas fault), it is known as a strike-slip fault.

Tremor: A low-intensity earthquake.

Volcano: A vent in the Earth's crust from which lava and other materials are ejected; also, a mountain that has been built up by lava and other material.

Geologic time

Scientists have divided geologic time into different intervals, with eras covering the longest spans of time and epochs the shortest. These divisions were determined by the relative positions of sedimentary rocks and by the types of fossils found in those rocks. The eras were the first to be determined. Then, as more data were gathered and rock-dating techniques were refined, the eras were divided into periods; the periods, in turn, were partitioned into epochs. Finally, with the development of isotopic dating, years were assigned to each time interval. The main geologic time divisions appear below, with the oldest units at the bottom of the scale and the most recent at the top.

Era	Period	Epoch	Years Ago
Cenozoic	Quaternary	Holocene	0 to 10,000
		Pleistocene	10,000 to 2 million
	Tertiary	Pliocene	2-5 million
		Miocene	5-24 million
		Oligocene	24-37 million
		Eocene	37-58 million
		Paleocene	58-66 million
Mesozoic	Cretaceous		66-144 million
	Jurassic		144-208 million
	Triassic		208-245 million
Paleozoic	Permian		245-286 million
	Carboniferous		
	Pennsylvanian		286-315 million
	Mississippian		315-360 million
	Devonian		360-408 million
	Silurian		408-438 million
	Ordovician		438-505 million
	Cambrian		505-570 million
Pre-cambrian	Proterozoic		570 million to 2.5 billion
	Archeozoic		2.5-4.6 billion

Index

Staff for
UNDERSTANDING SCIENCE & NATURE

Editorial Directors: Patricia Daniels, Allan Fallow, Karin Kinney
Writer: Mark Galan
Assistant Editor/Research: Elizabeth Thompson
Editorial Assistant: Louisa Potter
Production Manager: Prudence G. Harris
Senior Copy Coordinator: Jill Lai Miller
Production: Celia Beattie
Library: Louise D. Forstall
Computer Composition: Deborah G. Tait (Manager), Monika D.
   Thayer, Janet Barnes Syring, Lillian Daniels

Special Contributors, Text: Marfé Ferguson Delano,
   Margery duMond, Barbara Mallen, Gina Maranto,
   Greg Mock, Mark Washburn
Design/Illustration: Antonio Alcalá, Caroline Brock, Nicholas
   Fasciano, Catherine D. Mason, David Neal Wiseman
Photography: Cover: Lee Allen Thomas/Douglas Peebles Photogra-
   phy. Title page: Paul Chesley/Photographers Aspen. 12: National
   Park Service. 16: NASA. 45: U.S. Geological Survey; Haleakela
   National Park. 59: U.S. Navy. 68: Crater Lake National Park.
   78: U.S. Geological Survey. 80: National Park Service. 84, 85:
   Yellowstone National Park. 87: Richard Tollo. 131: UPI/
   Bettmann. 133: NASA
Research: Eugenia Scharf
Index: Barbara L. Klein

Consultants:

Dr. George Stephens is chairman of the geology department at
George Washington University in Washington, D.C. He special-
izes in structural geology.
Dr. Richard Tollo, an assistant professor of geology at George
Washington University, specializes in granites and the geology of
the central Appalachian Mountains.

Library of Congress Cataloging-in-Publication Data
Planet earth.
      p.   cm. — (Understanding science & nature; 8)
   Summary: Questions and answers explore the shape and structure
of the Earth, continental drift and plate tectonics, earthquakes, volcanoes, oceans, and other aspects of our world.
   ISBN 0-8094-9666-6 (trade) — ISBN 0-8094-9667-4 (lib. bdg.)
   1. Earth—Juvenile literature.
   [1. Earth—Miscellanea.   2. Questions and answers.]
I. Time-Life Books.   II. Series.
QB631.4.P53   1992
550—dc20   92-270
                                               CIP
                                                AC

TIME-LIFE for CHILDREN ™

Publisher: Robert H. Smith
Associate Publisher and Managing Editor: Neil Kagan
Assistant Managing Editor: Patricia Daniels
Editorial Directors: Jean Burke Crawford, Allan Fallow,
   Karin Kinney, Sara Mark, Elizabeth Ward
Director of Marketing: Margaret Mooney
Product Managers: Cassandra Ford, Shelley L. Schimkus
Director of Finance: Lisa Peterson
Financial Analyst: Patricia Vanderslice
Administrative Assistant: Barbara A. Jones
Special Contributor: Jacqueline A. Ball

Original English translation by International Editorial Services Inc.
C. E. Berry

Second printing 1993. Printed in U.S.A.
Published simultaneously in Canada.
School and library distribution by Time-Life Education,
P.O. Box 85026, Richmond, Virginia 23285-5026.
Time Life Inc. is a wholly owned subsidiary of
THE TIME INC. BOOK COMPANY.
TIME-LIFE is a trademark of Time Warner Inc. U.S.A.
For subscription information, call 1-800-621-7026.